TEENAGE YEARS

Written and illustrated by Beverly Guhl

Co-Author of Purrfect Parenting

FISHER
BOOKS

Library of Congress Cataloging-in-Publication Data
Guhl, Beverly, 1952-
    Teenage years : a parent's survival guide / by Beverly Guhl.
        p.   cm.
    Includes bibliographical references.
    ISBN 1-55561-027-7
        1. Teenagers—United States—Family relationships. 2. Parenting—
United States . 3. Communication in the family—United States.
4. Parent and child—United States. 5. Teenagers—Canada—Family
relationships. 6. Parenting— Canada. 7. Communication in the
family—Canada. 8. Parent and child—Canada.   I. Title.
HQ796.G84   1989
649'.125—dc20   89-17243
                                                        CIP

Publishers: Bill Fisher, Helen Fisher, Howard Fisher, Tom Monroe, P.E.
Editor: Judith Schuler
Electronic Type: Anne Olson

Published by Fisher Books
PO Box 38040
Tucson, Arizona 85740-8040
(602) 292-9080

Very special, super-duper thanks to some very special, super-duper people:
Rosalyn Rosen, M.S., B.S.S.W.
Catalina Herrerias, M.S.W., Ph.D.
Don Johnson, Ph.D.
Bill Edwards, M.S.
Blake Williams
Jon Guhl
Asa Guhl
God—Credentials too lengthy to list here
And Judi Schuler, the Fishers, Pat Barnes, Lynette Williams, Susan Rhodes, Betty Williams, Nan Richardson, Gary Guhl, Peter Markham, Joe Scruggs and bunches of others.

This book is very warmly dedicated to all post-adolescents and their adolescents!

Any resemblance to actual adolescent or post-adolescent unpersons is an unintentionally contrived coincidence.

No names have been changed to protect the guilty and/or paranoid.

The pronoun "he" is used rampantly throughout this book. Its use does not infer discrimination or incrimination.

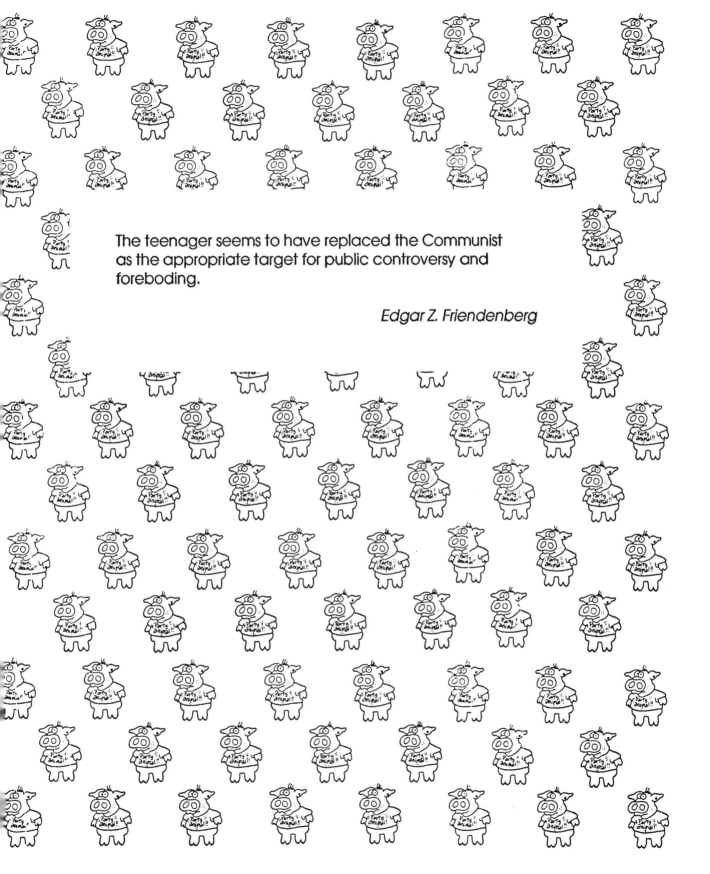

The teenager seems to have replaced the Communist as the appropriate target for public controversy and foreboding.

Edgar Z. Friendenberg

A challenge to the author from a "concerned" parent.

I'VE READ OTHER BOOKS ON PARENTING, AND THEY'RE ALL THE SAME. WE DON'T NEED ANOTHER HOTSHOT KNOW-IT-ALL LIKE YOU TRYING TO TELL US ABOUT PROBLEMS AND BATTLES WITH TEENAGERS. WE'RE LIVING IT EVERY DAY WITH OUR TEENAGERS. WE NEED TO KNOW WHAT TO *DO* ABOUT IT! I HOPE THERE'S SOME *SERIOUS HELP* IN THIS BOOK AND SOME *TECHNIQUES* TO USE. SOMETHING! ANYTHING! PLEASE!!!

BEVERLY GUHL

Dear Concerned Parent:

You'll be happy to know this book is loaded with helpful insight, sound child-psychology principles and proven, easy-to-use "lifesaving" techniques you can really sink your teeth into! I've got two teenagers of my own, ages 15 and 17, so I've experienced many of the same situations you have. But don't be fooled by the humorous format. All I did was to take serious psychological mumbo jumbo and put it into the entertaining, "yawnproof" format you see here. It wasn't a pretty job, but somebody had to do it.

Happy reading!

Beverly Guhl

UNIVERSAL AXIOMS OF 'TEENOLOGY'...

AXIOM NUMBER ONE

ONE CHILD IS NOT ENOUGH,
BUT ONE TEEN IS WAY TOO MANY.

AXIOM NUMBER TWO

YOU CAN TAKE THE TEEN OUT OF THE PARTY,
BUT YOU CAN'T TAKE THE PARTY OUT OF THE TEEN.

AXIOM NUMBER THREE

IF PARENTS DON'T GIVE TEENS JUST CAUSE
TO REBEL, TEENS WON'T REBEL "JUST 'CAUSE.*"

*hopefully.

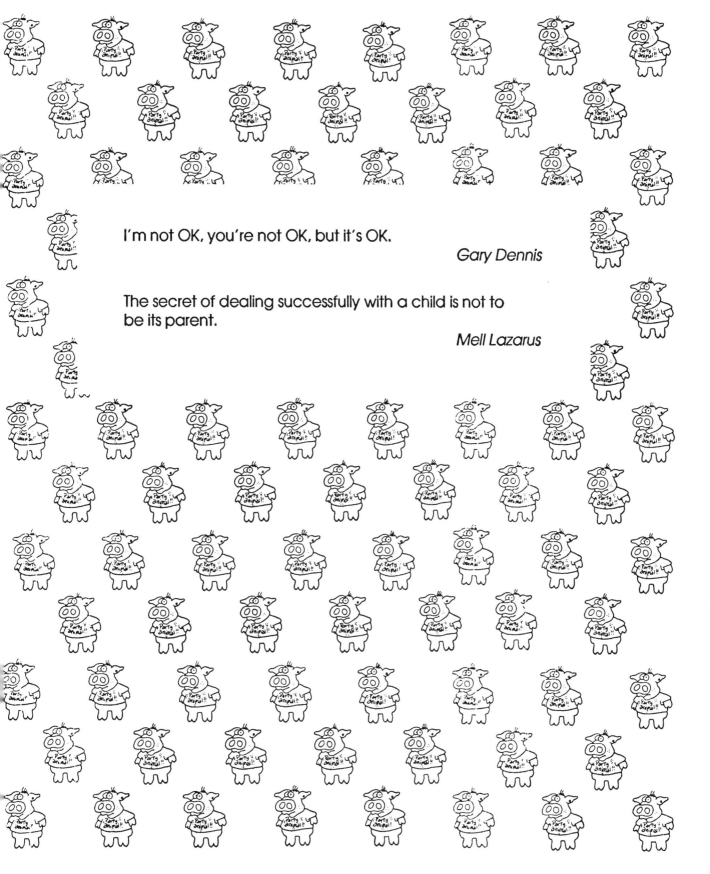

I'm not OK, you're not OK, but it's OK.

Gary Dennis

The secret of dealing successfully with a child is not to
be its parent.

Mell Lazarus

YOU ARE NOT ALONE!

The voyage from diaper rash to dealing with hash is an all-too-quick one. It catches parents off-guard and ill-prepared! While some parents cope fairly well with their teenager, others are serving 5 to 10 for assault with intent to disassemble.

It's consoling to know, in spite of everything, most teenagers turn out all right! This may seem dubious in your neck of the galaxy right now, but you turned out all right. (You did, didn't you?)

6

Nevertheless, we sit alone in the dark, waiting and hoping for the teenager to come home on time (or to come home at all). We wonder what to do, how the whole mess started—and most important—if the cleaners can get the stain off our new slacks.

Before you can fix something, you have to understand how it works. Let's see how this whole mess started.

SPARR WARS

OUR STORYTELLER

Long ago, in a far-out galaxy, a couple decided to clone themselves (have kids). They did this with many preconceived notions, absolute expectations and heavy-duty vibes. Like all parents, their goal was to raise kids who'd become responsible, independent, well-adusted adults—with whom they would also be friends. They were also determined to be better parents than their parents had been!

Everything was cool for the first 11 years. Then almost overnight the scene was changed by something weird that appeared in the home stretch of their parenthood. It was . . . (background music please—the soundtrack to *2001*, *Jaws* and *The Twilight Zone*) . . . *a teenager!*

Not wanting all their years of awesomeness to go down the tubes, they decided to declare war! They considered passively waiting it out till their teen turned 18, like some parents do, but our heroes were too hip for that! They believed parental methods, no matter how suspect, are always justified by the noble cause—like answers "blowing in the wind"—as the folk lyrics go.

Their artillery had always been their laser-like minds, screaming voices, physical and psychological dominance, authority and total *control*. With all that going for them, they were sure to win. They believed all they had to do was use these weapons and tactics with greater frequency and force.

However, the situation only escalated. Everyone scored emotional victories and defeats simultaneously. The effects lingered for hours (maybe even lifetimes)! A peaceful solution had to be found before they all nuked their happiness, sanity and love for each other off the face of the earth. But how?

Was peace possible or even normal? These parents had given it their best shot, and nothing worked!

What were they supposed to do?

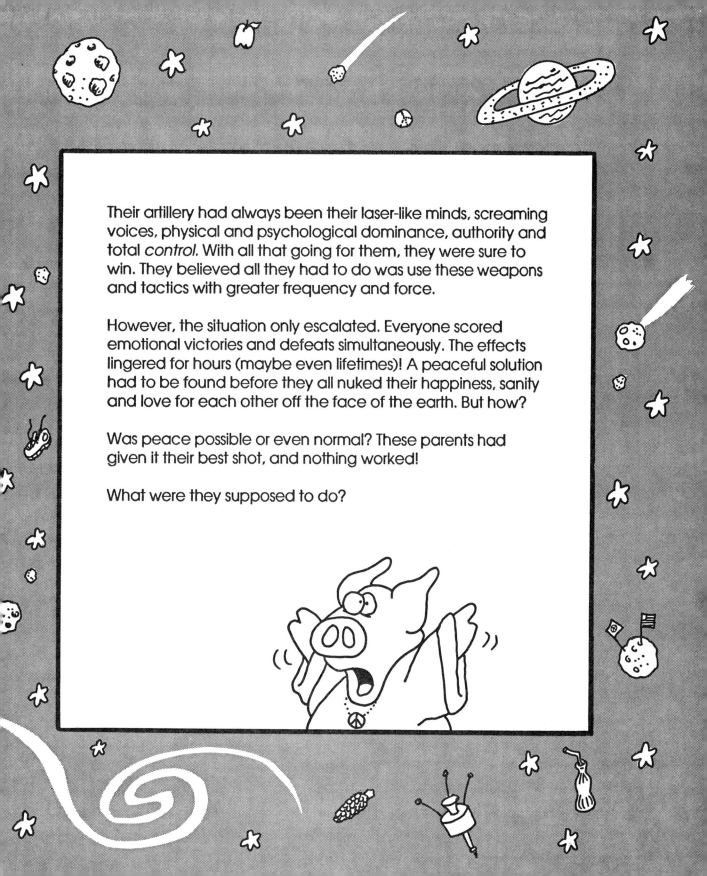

"What's a parent to do?"

Parents are the *key* to this mystery and the *solution* to the problem. No, this isn't an intergalactic guilt trip. You're not solely to blame for the whole mess, but you do have more responsibility and "control" in the mess than you probably realize!

Good intentions, personal expectations, preconceived notions and outdated approaches are no match for coping with one of the most unique species in the universe—*your* teenager! Dealing with a teenager requires attitudinal reprogramming, consistency, user-friendly communication skills and proven techniques interfaced with a common-sense, respectful and loving approach. So, smile.

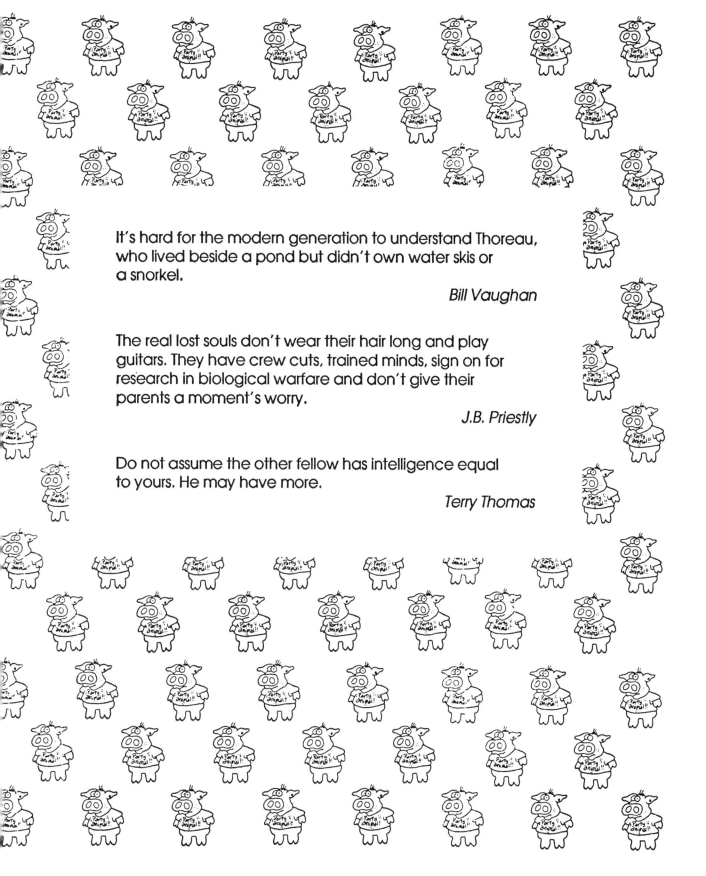

It's hard for the modern generation to understand Thoreau,
who lived beside a pond but didn't own water skis or
a snorkel.

Bill Vaughan

The real lost souls don't wear their hair long and play
guitars. They have crew cuts, trained minds, sign on for
research in biological warfare and don't give their
parents a moment's worry.

J.B. Priestly

Do not assume the other fellow has intelligence equal
to yours. He may have more.

Terry Thomas

HOW COULD YOU BE SO STUPID?? I DIDN'T ASK WHAT WAS WRONG WITH TEENAGERS IN THE 1950's AND 60's!!!...

Hmmm... COULD THIS MEAN THE WAY EACH GENERATON OF ADULTS VIEWS TEENAGERS MAY BE OPINIONATED, PREJUDICIAL AND STEREOTYPICAL? IF ANOTHER'S BEHAVIOR, TASTES AND ATTITUDES DIFFER FROM OURS OR THEY DON'T MEASURE UP TO OUR INFALLIBLE STANDARDS, EXPECTATIONS AND NOTIONS, DOES IT MEAN THEY ARE WRONG AND/OR INFERIOR TO US?? ALWAYS!!!...(ha! just kidding!!)... BUT WAIT A MINUTE... ISN'T OUR TEENAGER ANOTHER PERSON, TOO? WHAT MAKES 'OUR TEENAGER' ANY DIFFERENT FROM 'ANOTHER PERSON,' OR EVEN FROM US ???... WHAT THE HECK IS A TEENAGER ANYWAY ?????!...

WARNING: THE FOLLOWING SHOULD NOT BE READ BY PARENTS WITH WEAK HEARTS OR CLOSED MINDS...

WHAT IS A TEENAGER?

Living proof that MOTHER NATURE has a sense of humor?!

A teenager is an "adolescent." Adolescence is a unique process—a roller-coaster ride out of childhood into adulthood. The ticket is purchased around age 11 or 12—nobody gets off before the ride is over! Unwilling passengers (parents) are advised to bring a plain brown paper bag for the ride.

You can make the best of it by recognizing and respecting the necessity of the teen's ride. Let go with both hands, and experience the frightening exhilaration that comes with encouraging your teen to successfully complete the ride into adulthood, as he must. Parents who try to aggressively steer the teen are in for an unusually rough ride.

ANATOMY OF A TEENAGER

1. **Brain**—Infinitely clever and complex. By age 15, adult intelligence is reached. Excellent memory functions—able to store parental mistakes for lifetime recall.

2. **Hair**—Often worn in unique style or color preferred by teen or peers. Usually contrary to fuddy-duddy parental tastes. Visible manifestation of teen rebellion or of teen's right to self-expression of his own tastes and values—or both!

3. **Eyes**—Usually see only what they want to see or what they're allowed to see (experience) for themselves.

4. **Ears**—Hear only what they want to hear. Partial, transitory hearing loss is indigenous to adolescence. (Improved hearing returns in early 20s.) Ears often pierced—one ear for guys, both for gals.

5. **Nose**—Able to smell fun, beer, marijuana and "rats" (tattletale siblings), party-pooper peers or nosey parents about to meddle in teen's life.

6. **Mouth**—Used for arguing or fighting for rights as a person. Sometimes also used for consumption of alcohol, tobacco and drugs—just like adult mouths!

7. **Skin**—Very thick, sometimes justifiably so. Occasionally garnished with real tattoos or safety pins (yowie).

8. **Heart**—Very pliable. Easily broken, and hard, but not impossible, to repair.

9. **Arms**—Used for gesticulation. Also used by parents to grab onto to gain attention or halt spontaneous, unexcused teen departures.

10. **Stomach**—A bottomless junk-food pit. Gastric distress fairly common. Parents are a major source of distress. Secondary sources include school, society, opposite sex and alcohol.

11. **Clothing**—Usually style teen and peers prefer. Mode of self-expression and/or peer acceptance. May also be used as a means of rebellion. Designer labels often deemed "essential."

12. **Body changes**—Girls get curvier; boys get hunkier. Physical changes echo internal changes. Very powerful hormonal forces at work. Confusing and frustrating to teens and parents. Source of much anxiety and rebellion for one and all!

A TEENAGER IS NOT:

A child
A slave
A carbon copy or clone of either parent
A helpless creature requiring constant adult
    attention
A superior being "entitled" to anything and
    everything it wants
An inferior life form due to age, size, I.Q. or earning
    power
An untrustworthy criminal requiring constant supervision and restriction

A TEENAGER IS:

A young adult
A totally unique person unto itself/himself/herself
A responsive human being with needs and
    personal values
A biological creature undergoing hormonal and
    physiological changes
A person experiencing brain growth and adult
    thought processes
A person of human worth and dignity equal to that of any
    human being
A maturing individual whom Nature is compelling to become independent

WHAT'S THE DIFF ??...

Important—Your attitude, perception and expectations of your teenager are the foundation on which your relationship is built. It directly affects how you deal with him, as well as how the teen responds to you. Most of the mistakes parents make with their teen are the direct result of not treating him with mutual respect.

To illustrate this important point, let's play the *What-if* game.

WHAT IF your spouse treated you as if you were a teenager?

WHAT IF   your neighbor treated you as if you were a teenager?

WHAT IF   your boss treated you as if you were a teenager?

WHAT IF your best friend treated you as if you were a teenager?

In each of the situations shown above, how would you feel? You're a mature adult, yet you'd probably feel angry, humiliated, frustrated, rebellious and despairing. Is it any wonder a teenager (young adult) feels the same way?

You can't begin to be an effective parent to a teenager if you don't see the teenager as a separate human being worthy of your respect. You must treat him with human dignity and trust, the same way you treat your friends. Acknowledge he is your equal in his right and ability to run his own life (especially the older he gets) instead of being controlled by you!

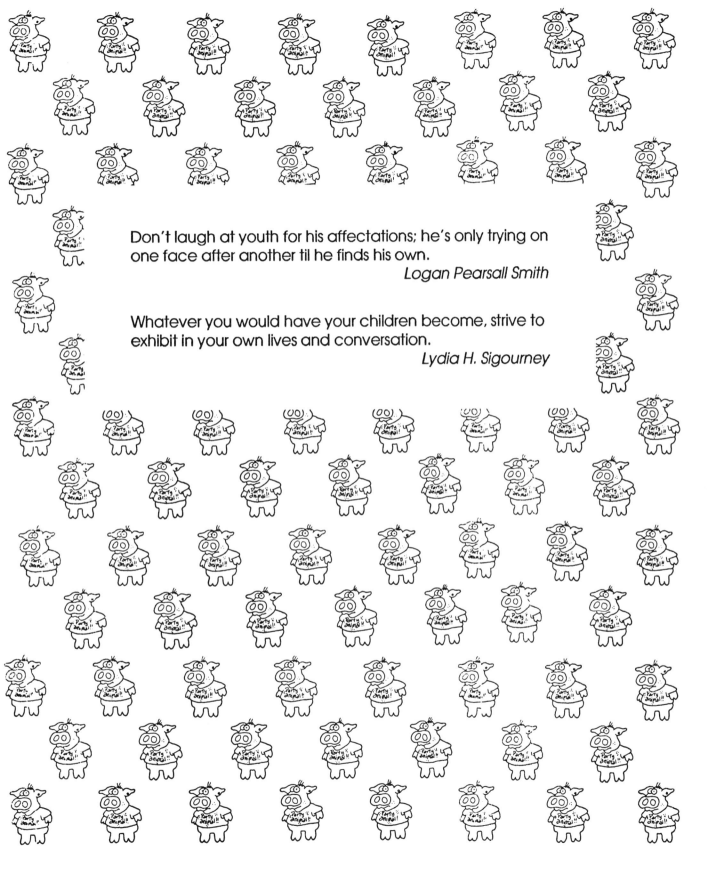

Don't laugh at youth for his affectations; he's only trying on one face after another til he finds his own.

Logan Pearsall Smith

Whatever you would have your children become, strive to exhibit in your own lives and conversation.

Lydia H. Sigourney

It's not NICE to mess with Mother Nature!!

Teen behavior is something Mother Nature is compelling them to do! Crazy but true; it's a sign of normal human development and sound mental health to have an assertive, biologically activated teenager running around the house. Besides being normal, behavior also serves vitally important purposes too! (Does the irony never end?) These purposes have positive and negative attributes—sometimes which is which is merely a matter of perception!

THE GOOD -- Their behavior enables teens to "find themselves," achieve self-worth, gain peer acceptance, form their own opinions and values, and practice interacting in the "real world" they will one day independently be a part of.

THE BAD AND THE UGLY -- These same testing-their-wings behaviors often result in adverse side effects—clashes with people of opposing viewpoints and opinions (parents, teachers, others). These clashes take shape in rebellion, manipulative behaviors and power struggles. But don't blame the teen—blame Mother Nature and your spouse's genes and our culture and . . . you name it!

MONKEY SEE, MONKEY DO! -- a.k.a. Copycatting; Role Modeling

TEENS CAN FOLLOW **CLASS** ACTS AS EASILY AS **CRASS** ACTS!!

Teens are shopping for their own identity and values like a new pair of clothes. They'll look to see what's in style, what peers and others are wearing and what you're wearing. What doesn't fit is quickly or eventually discarded.

The behavior you model can influence your teen to not believe what you say, to smoke, drink, lie, cheat, steal, do drugs, be physically abusive, be hypocritical, prejudiced, underachieving, uncommunicative, unforgiving, lazy—or—to be kind, charitable, patient, unbiased, motivated, communicative, thoughtful, well-organized and so forth!

Teens need models not critics—especially not hypocrites!

THE HYPOCRITIC MOTTO--
Do as I say, not as I do!

DIDN'T I TELL YOU NOT TO FIGHT WITH PEOPLE ??!! I GUESS I'M GONNA HAVE TO BEAT SOME MORE SENSE INTO YOU !!!

IF I EVER CATCH YOU DATING A BLUE CAT AGAIN I'LL SKIN YOU ALIVE.!!! NOW... GET TO BED, WE'VE GOT CHURCH TOMORROW MORNING!!!

YOUR TEACHER SAYS YOU WERE CAUGHT CHEATING ON YOUR FINALS!! HOW COULD YOU? WHERE ARE YOUR MORALS? I'M SO ASHAMED! I THOUGHT I RAISED YOU BETTER THAN THIS!!!

WHAT ABOUT YOU??! YOU'VE GOT A RADAR DETECTOR ON YOUR COLLAR, YOU CHEAT ON YOUR TAXES, YOU TELL WHITE LIES TO YOUR FRIENDS, AND YOU GIVE KICKBACKS IN YOUR BUSINESS!!! YOU'RE THE BIGGEST CHEETAH I KNOW!!!

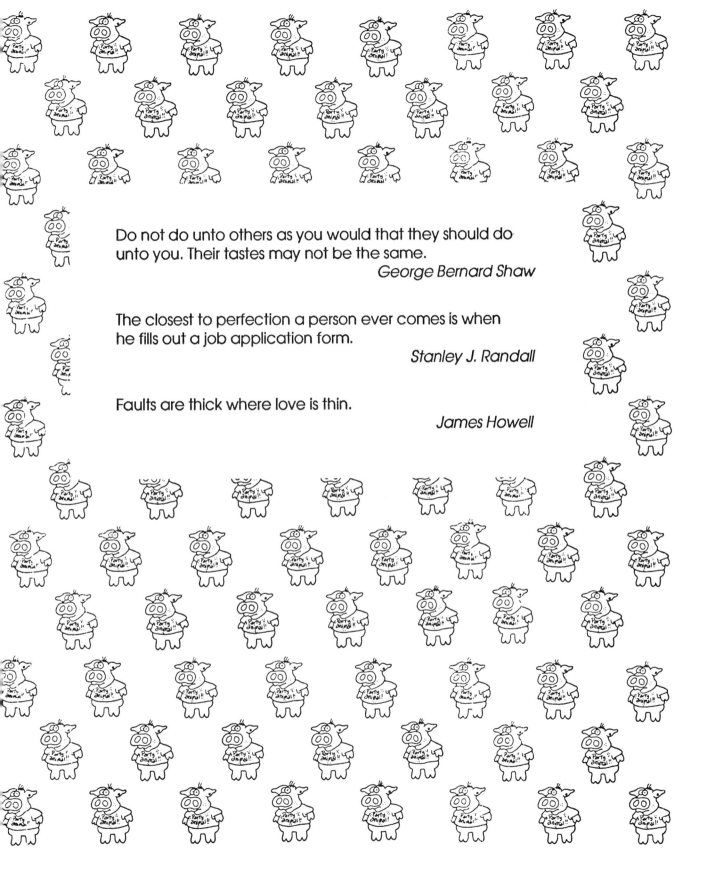

Do not do unto others as you would that they should do unto you. Their tastes may not be the same.

George Bernard Shaw

The closest to perfection a person ever comes is when he fills out a job application form.

Stanley J. Randall

Faults are thick where love is thin.

James Howell

EXPECTATIONS -- GREAT AND OTHERWISE

Everyone has certain novel expectations for his or her offspring. Expectations are the yardstick by which you measure your teenager and gauge your effectiveness as a parent! If the teen fails to measure up, you may feel like a loser. You may give up in disgust or try even harder to get the teen to conform. The teen, sensing disapproval, may rebel, try to conform or feel inadequate and give up on himself. Your expectations can be a powerful influence in your teen's life and in your relationship with him. Expectations come in two versions—unrealistic and realistic.

...THE 'SCIENCE FICTION' VERSION...

Unrealistic expectations are based on your ambitions or goals and do not take into consideration the personal ambitions, abilities and interests of your teen. If you're only focused on what you want your teen to do or become, you will never really understand and appreciate him for the unique person he is.

Wise up! . . . Whose life is it anyway?

...THE NON-FICTION VERSION...

Expecting the teen to become his or her own person, to be well-adjusted, socially acceptable, responsible, independent and perform reasonable tasks are all healthy, *realistic expectations* you should have for your teen!

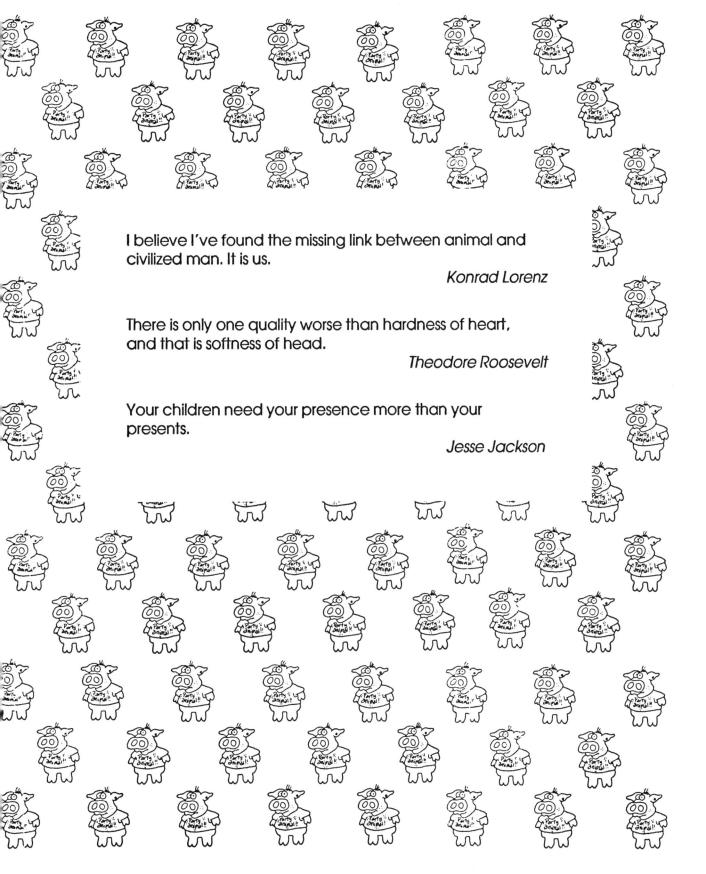

I believe I've found the missing link between animal and civilized man. It is us.

Konrad Lorenz

There is only one quality worse than hardness of heart, and that is softness of head.

Theodore Roosevelt

Your children need your presence more than your presents.

Jesse Jackson

WHOOO ARE YOU ??

You didn't stop being a person the minute you took on the stereotypical role of being a parent, did you? How can you tell? Are you behaving like two different people? Are you relaxed, friendly, kind and fun around your friends but totally different around your teenager? Chances are your teen is doing likewise!

Your teen is fast becoming an adult with whom you can more easily relate and enjoy as a new friend, if you'd try being yourself more often! Making the transition from icemaker (parent) to icebreaker (friend) is awkward for both at first but very rewarding!

And who knows—behind those strange clothes and underneath that weird haircut may lurk someone you may genuinely like!

ALL YOU NEED IS LOVE?...

Love conquers all, right? Wrong. Love is deaf, dumb, blind and stupid! Even wars have been fought in the name of love! Still, love with all its sweet imperfections is an essential, underlying motivation for most parents, as are good intentions and the fear of social humiliation!

♥ the tradeoff...

Some parents trade love for discipline. They feel so compelled to do whatever they perceive as parental duty to their teen that they are willing to forgo being loved, appreciated and respected in return.

Others trade discipline for love. They act more like contestants in a popularity contest than parents! They so desperately want their teen (stepteen?) to love or at least like them that they are willing to forgo consistency and even necessary discipline! (Catch 22—Failure to discipline or set limits is often interpreted by the teen as a sign you don't really love or care about him!)

♥ the payoff...

Some parents demonstrate love through giving, doing and purchasing power for their teen. But that teaches the teen to equate love with parental enslavement and money! He will expect more such "love." This leads to manipulation, guilt, ingratitude and hassles.

♥ the Kiss off...

As one philosopher put it so well, you can pick your friends and your nose, but you can't pick your relatives! In spite of everything, there are no guarantees you're going to like or love your kids, that they're going to like each other or us, or they'll even turn out to be likable people!

Heredity and/or environment? It's tough to say. There are lots of weird genes floating around, and teens are also floating around being exposed to various influences here, there and everywhere!

SOW'S EARS?

If you find yourself (temporarily?) incompatible with your teen, what should you do?

  Acknowledge to yourself your teen is a "pig." (Your opinion!)

 Let go of your feelings, and stop feeling guilty or sad. Guilt and sadness won't change anything. (See Attitude, pages 45 to 56.)

 Find some positive things about the teen, and appreciate those! (See Encouragement, pages 106 to 108.)

Don't let your incompatibility interfere with your responsibilities to the teen or the teen's basic human/civil rights.

 Stay open-minded. Teens are an evolutionary organism. Today's sow's ear may be tomorrow's silk purse!

34

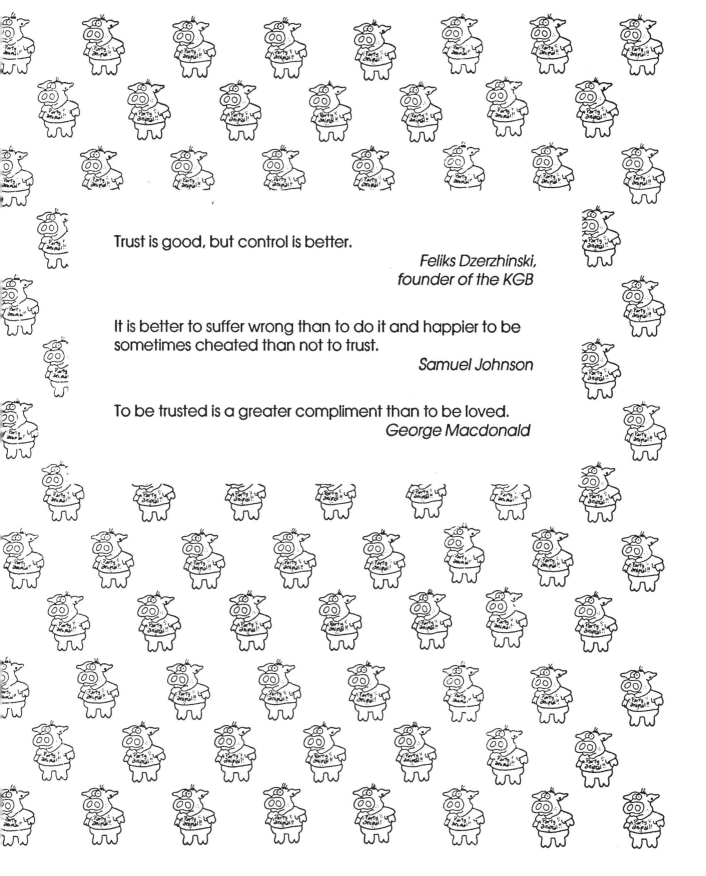

Trust is good, but control is better.

Feliks Dzerzhinski,
founder of the KGB

It is better to suffer wrong than to do it and happier to be
sometimes cheated than not to trust.

Samuel Johnson

To be trusted is a greater compliment than to be loved.
George Macdonald

HELLO, FOLKS!! Ed McHam here! The results of our "PARENTS CLEARINGHOUSE CONTEST" are in!! As you know, TEEN CONTESTANTS were asked to send in their proven methods for "dealing with" their parents! Contestants amazed, even disgusted, us with their ingenuity, cunning and resourcefulness! Let's meet the WINNERS...

Contestant #1: Artie Dodger

I can dodge chores and things by telling my parents I have too much homework or an important TEST the next day or I HAVE to be somewhere. OR I try to NOT BE AROUND when I know it's time for me to do something, such as the dishes or clean up! I'm out fetching a Frizbee, chasing cars or something!!

Contestant #2: Vic Timm

I get my way by making my parents feel guilty or by appealing to their "competitive and social sensibilities!" All I have to do is tell them EVERYBODY ELSE gets to HAVE stuff or go places!! OR I say "IF YOU REALLY LOVE ME, YOU'LL...........!"--Works every time!

Contestant #3: Pixie Weakerwunn

I pick out which of my folks is the weaker target... My Mom is soft-headed, I mean soft-HEARTED!, so I ask her for most things! I've learned just what to say or how to act to get my way! Once I get Mom on my side, I use that to make Daddy cooperate, TOO!!!

Contestant #4: ZaZa Distractem

I FIND THE RIGHT MOMENT when one or BOTH of my folks is distracted or real busy, and I ask permission for something! Often they don't even KNOW what I've asked 'cause they're TOO DISTRACTED or just aren't paying enough attention anyway‼

Contestant #5: Merrilee Threatenzem

I THREATEN my parents with ALL KINDS OF THINGS -- everything from screaming, running away from home, suicide -- or taking them to COURT‼ They're so afraid I'LL DO something drastic that I usually get my way‼!

Contestant #6: Dee Bates

My parents always try to REASON with me! Because I'm so much SMARTER than they are, I can argue and debate everything they say! I deftly change the focus from MY behavior by pointing out how INCONSISTENT, IMPERFECT and HYPOCRITICAL THEY are! I love a good power game… I mean… debate‼

Contestant #7: Howie D'Coy

I use what I call the "D'COY" Method! I give 'em my decoy request FIRST, which they SHOOT DOWN… THEN I give 'em my REAL request -- which always looks modest by comparison‼ I say "Well, if I can't do THAT, then can I at least do THIS…?" They think it's a _fair_ compromise, so they say OK‼

Contestant #8: Vera Helplezz

IF I ACT helpless and dependent, my parents feel sorry for me and will do things FOR me-- they help with my homework or make excuses for me and don't expect a whole lot from me! I kinda enjoy this... I may keep this up till I'm 30!!

Contestant #9: Willie Reevenge

My parents are so unfair and overpowering, all I can do is find ways to score with revenge!! It's great to know I can FRUSTRATE them, too! Oh, sure, they pay me back for paying them back, but isn't that what life's all about--"do unto others?"

...GRAND PRIZE WINNER!!!...

Contestant #10: Ruff Tuff

My parents don't give me no *8%#! I bought a gun, and they know @#%& WELL I'LL USE IT too!! I can come and go as I please. I got my freedom, my drugs, my booze:...MAN!, I GOT IT MADE!! I ain't NEVER leavin' home!!!!

(Judge's note—Solutions for counteracting these winning methods are found throughout this book.)

TEST YOUR PARENTAL POWERS!!!

HOW MUCH CONTROL or POWER CAN YOU EXERT OVER YOUR TEENAGER???!!!!!

Answer the following tricky questions YES or NO! ...

YES NO
☐ ☐ I CAN PREVENT MY TEENAGER FROM SEEING DIRTY MOVIES!
☐ ☐ I CAN MAKE MY TEENAGER DRIVE SAFELY!
☐ ☐ I CAN BE WITH MY TEENAGER AT SCHOOL!
☐ ☐ I CAN PREVENT MY TEENAGER FROM DRINKING or USING DRUGS!
☐ ☐ I CAN MAKE MY TEENAGER APPRECIATE LAWRENCE WELK!
☐ ☐ I CAN ALWAYS BE SURE MY TEENAGER IS TELLING THE TRUTH!
☐ ☐ I CAN PREVENT MY TEENAGER FROM RIDING WITH DRUNK DRIVERS!
☐ ☐ I CAN PREVENT MY TEENAGER FROM HAVING SEX!
☐ ☐ I CAN HEAL MY TEENAGER'S HEART WHEN IT'S 'BROKEN'!
☐ ☐ I CAN PREVENT MY TEENAGER FROM USING BAD LANGUAGE!
☐ ☐ I CAN MAKE MY TEENAGER LISTEN TO SLIM WHITMAN RECORDS!
☐ ☐ I CAN PREVENT MY TEENAGER FROM GETTING AIDS!

...answers on following page!...

IF YOU ANSWERED YES TO ANY OF THE QUESTIONS: YOU LOSE !!!!

The bubble-bursting fact is control is strictly an illusion. You have no real control over what your teen thinks, likes, feels or where he really goes, what he really does or even what happens to him! You can't be with him every second. You can't monitor his every phone call, movement, heartbeat or brain wave.

Note—Some argue control can be achieved, citing their own "proven methods"—guilt induction, humiliation, screaming, threats, name-calling, intimidation, striking, spanking, grounding, imprisonment, brainwashing, torture. Scoff, scoff!

One doesn't achieve control by such methods. One achieves resentment, hostility, rebellion, runaways, alienation of affection and worse! Any "compliance" elicited by such means is superficial, incidental and limited. Even the most controlling parent can't be with his teen 24 hours a day or control what he's thinking!

All you can ever really do is assume, hope, trust and have varying degrees of influence on your offspring—things you need to continue to do. How? Let's find out. As Francis Bacon said, "Knowledge is power!" (The right kind!)

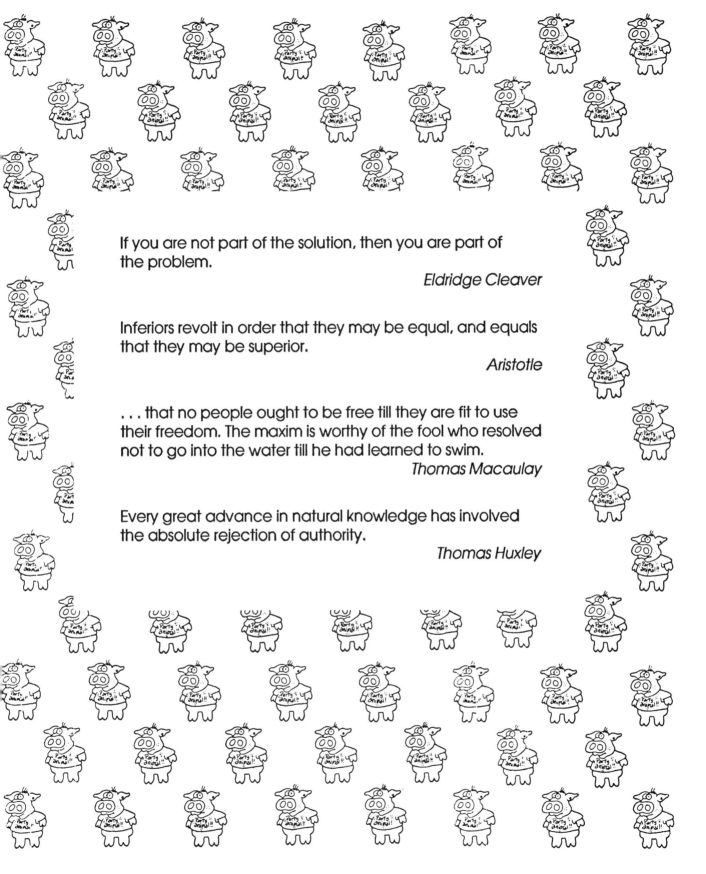

If you are not part of the solution, then you are part of the problem.

Eldridge Cleaver

Inferiors revolt in order that they may be equal, and equals that they may be superior.

Aristotle

. . . that no people ought to be free till they are fit to use their freedom. The maxim is worthy of the fool who resolved not to go into the water till he had learned to swim.

Thomas Macaulay

Every great advance in natural knowledge has involved the absolute rejection of authority.

Thomas Huxley

BREAKING TRAINING

Having acknowledged and accepted the fact you can't control your teenager (or anyone else), yet knowing there are things you need to get him to stop, look, listen and do—how can you train your teenager to respond to you? The same way you've been training him not to respond to you!

ROCKY'S REBELLION

42

By not allowing Rocky to run his own life, his parents give Rocky a reason to rebel! The *purpose* of Rocky's rebellion is to struggle for control and seek revenge. The parents respond by *choosing* to feel angry and hurt—this is Rocky's reward/payoff for rebellion! Rocky's parents retaliated by severely punishing Rocky—which gives Rocky reason to rebel again!

The parents' responses, before and after the rebellion, teach Rocky the only way to solve his problems is through devious, manipulative means, not through love, communication and fair play. Sound familiar?

LIFECYCLE OF TEEN REBELLION

TO BREAK THE CYCLE:
1) STOP GIVING REASONS FOR REBELLION!
2) STOP RESPONDING INAPPROPRIATELY!

ATTITUDE-- IT'S ALL IN YOUR HEAD!

You can retrain your teenager and teach (influence) him to be better, or less bad, by changing your attitude and the way you interact with him. The key is to focus on yourself, what you can do, what you can change, how you feel and how you respond to your teenager.

It's not events (situations or teenagers) that affect you. It's what you tell yourself or believe about the event (or person) that determines how you respond, react, feel and behave. You can be happy or sad, smart or stupid, consistent or inconsistent, effective or ineffective, but it's your choice! In other words, your beliefs must get real before you can.

48

THE POWER OF CHOICE

ACTIVATING EVENT
(something happens!)

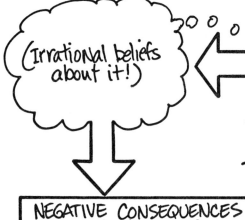

(Irrational beliefs about it!)

(Rational beliefs about it!)

the Person CHOOSES!

NEGATIVE CONSEQUENCES
(emotions/behavior)

GUILT	IMMOBILIZATION
ANGER	INCONSISTENCY
APATHY	INEFFECTIVENESS
DEPRESSION	POOR JUDGMENT
SADNESS	PROCRASTINATION
INFERIORITY	INTOLERANCE
PITY	UNFAIRNESS
HOSTILITY	IRRESPONSIBILITY
ANXIOUSNESS	AGGRESSION
LONELINESS	etc.
FEARFULNESS	
CONFUSION	
REJECTION	
etc.	

POSITIVE CONSEQUENCES
(emotions/behavior)

CONFIDENCE	ASSERTIVENESS
SELF-WORTH	CAPABLE
HAPPINESS	DIRECTED
ENJOYMENT	CONSISTENCY
PEACE	FAIRNESS
ACCEPTANCE	GROWTH
COMPASSION	FORGIVENESS
EMPATHY	RESPONSIBILITY
etc.	TOLERANCE
	FLEXIBILITY
*	COMMITMENT
	EFFECTIVENESS
	etc.

* VARYING DEGREES OF NEGATIVE EMOTIONS ARE THE NORMAL, AND UNAVOIDABLE, RESULT OF MANY RATIONAL BELIEFS AS WELL. OUR EMOTIONS ARE WHAT MAKES US ALIVE AND HUMAN--well, some of us, that is!!! THE **KEY** IS TO DO AWAY WITH AS MANY IRRATIONAL BELIEFS AS WE CAN SO WE WON'T HAVE TO EXPERIENCE ANY MORE 'NEGATIVE CONSEQUENCES' THAN WE ORDINARILY HAVE TO! NATURE PROVIDES US WITH ENOUGH HASSLES--WHY 'MANUFACTURE' OUR OWN??!!!!

The Guilt Train stops here!!

Engineers or passengers? It's vital to teach your teenager he also has this power of choice. If you don't, he'll try to railroad you (and others) into being responsible for how he feels and behaves. No riders please . . . Choo . . . Choo . . . Choose!

51

What's a parent to do if he or she isn't busy fostering dependency or inciting rebellion? Easy! Enjoy the well-deserved freedom that comes with letting the teenager assume his fair and rightful share of the problems, decisions and consequences for running his own life! This trains the teen to become a capable, responsible and confident adult, too!

WHY DIDN'T YOU WAKE ME UP? NOW I'M GOING TO BE LATE! YOU'LL HAVE TO DRIVE ME!!!

I'm not an alarm cock! He knows what time to get up; it's HIS responsibility and HIS problem!! He can suffer the consequences...

It's NOT a pig pen! It's so CLEAN! Oh well, I can't MAKE him keep it MESSY! I guess I can ask him to keep the door shut and not clean up elsewhere. I don't have to go in there either. It's HIS pen and HIS problem!

Keep OUT! XX ...or else!

I DON'T FEEL LIKE STUDYING! HOMEWORK SUCKS! ... JUST LEAVE ME ALONE!!!

WHAT A GRIZZLY SITUATION THIS IS!! I CAN'T FORCE him to study, and I'm not responsible for his homework, but I don't want to see him fail!! Nagging and punishing hasn't worked! I have to let go of his problem and let him be responsible. His grades may suffer and he'll get kicked off the team, or he may have to go to summer school or repeat a grade. But it's HIS CHOICE, unbearable as it may be!

When a problem or situation (activating event) occurs, stop and ask yourself, "Who owns this problem?" Believing you own the problem can be a rational or irrational belief—and you know what that means.

If the answer is largely "No," it's not your problem! Knowing who owns a problem helps determine the appropriate course of action or inaction. Sometimes you should simply withdraw, not get involved and let natural or logical consequences take over! At other times, you'll need to listen and offer encouragement and advice. Do this *only* if the advice is sought by the teen or if he's genuinely receptive to hearing it. When in doubt, check out his "receptivity."

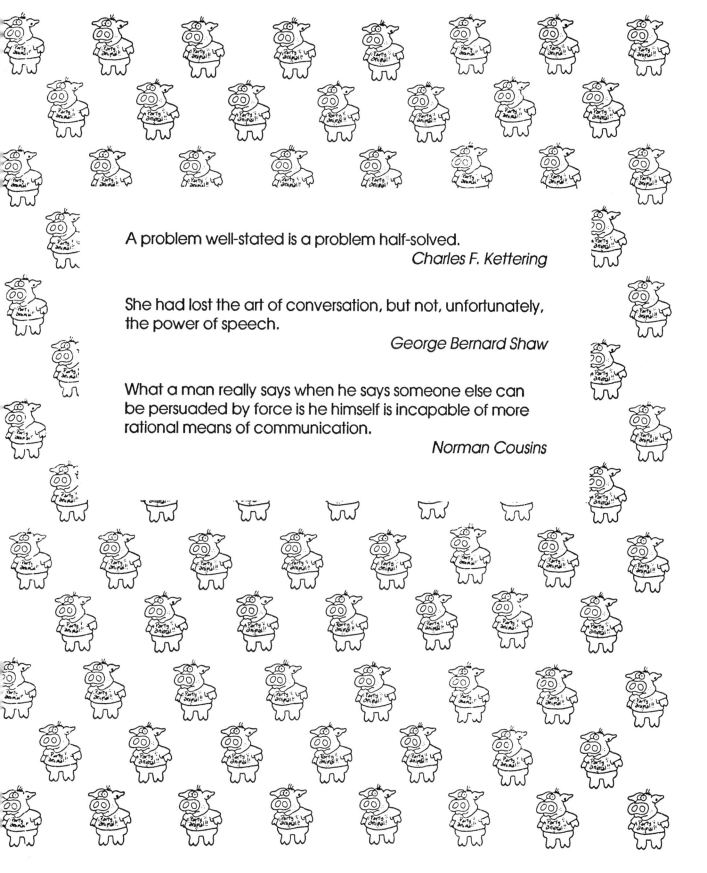

A problem well-stated is a problem half-solved.

Charles F. Kettering

She had lost the art of conversation, but not, unfortunately, the power of speech.

George Bernard Shaw

What a man really says when he says someone else can be persuaded by force is he himself is incapable of more rational means of communication.

Norman Cousins

Communication

Definition—The two-way system for the verbal and non-verbal transmission of feelings, needs, ideas, goals and expectations, which comprises the overall way we relate to and interact with one another.

TROUBLE ON THE LINES??...

Respectful communication is the key. Using simple communication skills (like those shown on the following pages) will help you connect with your teenager, even if all you've been getting is static or busy signals or if all the lines are down!

Note: The lines didn't break down overnight, and it may take a few weeks to repair them. So put your patience on hold, and hang in there!

EASY-ACCESS DIALING--

The first few *seconds* of any encounter are the most critical! Almost instantly you can sense one another's mood and attitude through facial expressions, eye contact (or lack of it), body language, demeanor, tone of voice and words. The way each of you acts (or reacts) can make the other defensive or receptive, cooperative or uncooperative, and so forth. It can even determine the likelihood of successful future encounters!

PARENTS DEMONSTRATING CONTACT IN SOME CLOSE ENCOUNTERS.

DOOMED ENCOUNTERS:

SUCCESSFUL ENCOUNTERS:

Why deprive your teen of his rightful responsibility (burden, hassle) to think and figure things out for himself or to be considerate of other's feelings and needs? The skills on the following pages show ways to "call forward" this responsibility to your teen, which will stimulate his brain into awareness (thinking, empathy) to produce results (listening, cooperation, cleaner rooms)!

OPERATOR ASSISTANCE..

Descriptive, factual statements or ones beginning with the word "I" safely keep the focus where it belongs—on the situation or behavior and/or your feelings. These statements don't attack the personality or character of the teen or imply guilt or blame. So they shouldn't put your teen on a high-voltage defense!

YUCK!

YES!!

YUCK!

YES!!

YUCK!

YES!!

THE PARTY LINE --

An occasional "we" sentence is pretty safe, too! It's got a quality of togetherness that's hard to beat! It conveys needs, but it's got a sneaky way of instilling morals, manners, values and other important concepts.

SPEED DIALING--

Like the convenience of a microwave oven, a *microsentence* can be a timesaver (and lifesaver). Teens also appreciate it. It's great when you're rushed or very mad. In this case, "less" accomplishes more!

TOUCH-TONE SERVICE--

In a friendly tone, direct your teen's attention to what needs to be done, and let him take the hint. Simply say his name or cough, grunt or clear your throat to get his attention. Then point to the item requiring his attention. Be nice, and don't forget to smile! No sense wasting a good snarl on trivial issues.

SORRY, WRONG NUMBER!

Avoid sentences beginning with or built around the word "you." That puts the blame or focus on the teen instead of on solving the problem. "You" has a loud, accusatory ring that can impair teen hearing and responses, as can any critical or angry sentence of any kind. Attack the problem, not the teen!

WHAT WE SAY ...	...WHAT OUR TEEN HEARS!!
Why haven't you mowed the lawn? *The lawn needs mowing.*	You're irresponsible and lazy. *The lawn needs to be mowed.*
You left a mess in the kitchen! *I need the kitchen kept clean.*	You're an inconsiderate slob! *The kitchen needs to be clean.*
Have you been drinking? *I hope you haven't been drinking.*	I don't trust you! *I care about you.*
Do as you're told. *What would you propose?*	Don't think. You have no rights. *I respect you as a person.*
Here's what you should do. *You'll do the right thing.*	You're helpless and incompetent. *You're capable and mature.*
Don't you have homework? *How's the report coming along?*	You're incapable of managing time. *I'm interested in you.*
Can't you do anything right? *Relax! Some things take time.*	You're inept, stupid and hopeless. *Nobody's perfect; you're doing fine.*
Your clothes look ridiculous! *What an interesting outfit.*	You have no taste. You're ridiculous. *You have a right to self-expression.*
How could you wreck the car? *We'll get an estimate tomorrow.*	You're a loser and a disappointment. *I understand; accidents happen.*

ANNOYANCE CALLS--

Too many "I" sentences are annoying to the teen and can make you sound selfish or egocentric. Alternate between the "I" and "we" sentences and the straight facts. Remember to be respectful. It's also OK to have fun.

VARIATIONS ON A THEME...

"OBSCENE" CALLS --

When your teen rings back with his own "I" sentences or "you" sentences (and he will), use active and reflective listening skills. (See pages 74 to 86.) Keep the focus on the present situation. For example, "We're not talking about the past; we're talking about this situation."

Note—Some days they're gonna "make your day," no matter how nice you try to be. Call on appropriate techniques and fair consequences as your backup. Always have a backup! (See page 104 and pages 144 to 146.)

COMMUNICATION CO-OP-- a.k.a. THE SWELL SYSTEM

"First do what needs to be done, then you can do what you want to do!" A first-things-first policy takes care of your needs (and/or what needs to be done), yet also recognizes the teen's needs (wants?). What could be more fair?

Whoa!!! ... NO NAGS!

Teens are notoriously skittish about nagging and hassling, thereby rendering it pretty ineffective, even harmful. Reminding merely teaches them not to be responsible for remembering things for themselves! Let your teen know he's responsible for remembering things and for any consequences of his forgetfulness! It's nice to break your teen in on low-risk consequences first, moving your way up to the heavy stuff!

In situations in which others could unfairly suffer from your teen's forgetfulness (baby-sitting clients, teachers, doctors, vets), communicate in ways to make the teen aware of other's needs. Occasionally use some subtle reminders.

THE YELLOW PAGES!
"LET YOUR FINGERS DO THE TALKING!"

Too tired or angry to speak? Your darling isn't anywhere in sight? Afraid you'll kill him when you do find him? Why preach it when you can post it? Leave a note!

Short and sweet, a note avoids confrontation and is appreciated by all. For big issues, a letter may be even better. (Teens can't interrupt or talk back to a note or letter.) When possible, make the message friendly and fun. Be sure to use notes and letters to say good things, too! Right? Write!

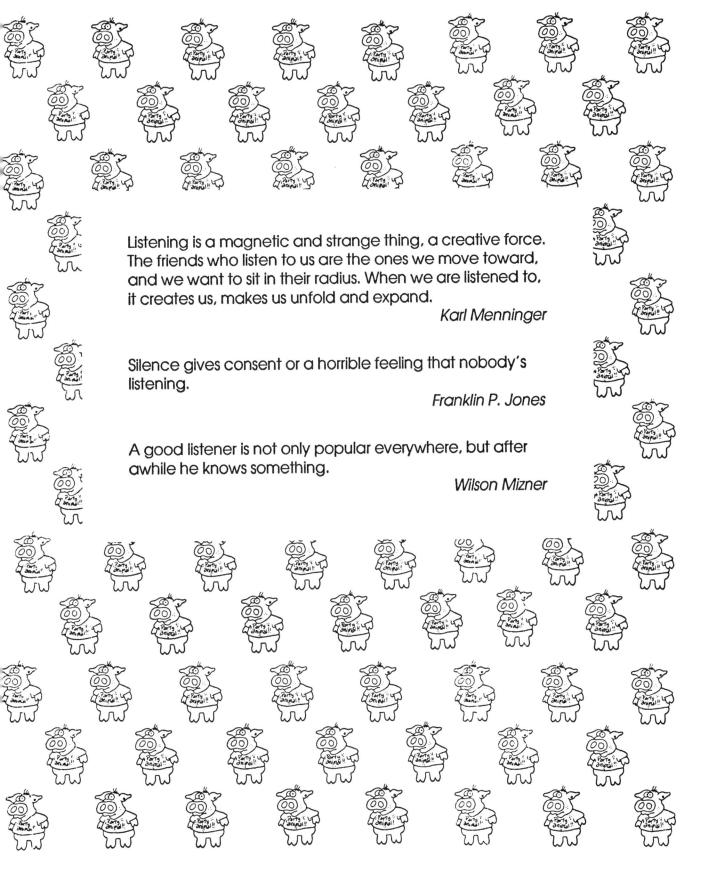

Listening is a magnetic and strange thing, a creative force. The friends who listen to us are the ones we move toward, and we want to sit in their radius. When we are listened to, it creates us, makes us unfold and expand.

Karl Menninger

Silence gives consent or a horrible feeling that nobody's listening.

Franklin P. Jones

A good listener is not only popular everywhere, but after awhile he knows something.

Wilson Mizner

listening

RING... RING... INCOMING MESSAGES...

The other crucial half of communication is *listening*. Teens transmit powerful messages through their emotions and behavior, as well as through their mouths. Picking up their feelings, words and meanings requires powers of hearing, seeing, sensing and thinking. (Shortcut to trouble—bypass the brain!)

TURN ON, TUNE IN! -- a.k.a. ACTIVE LISTENING

Sometimes all your teen wants is to be heard and feel you understand. He doesn't always want answers or conversation! Teens have this peculiar adult-like ability to sometimes solve their problems by simply talking about them to someone who'll listen! Your help and advice is often premature and unwelcomed!

So with faith and patient tongues, give your sincere, undivided attention. Make eye contact. Look for the non-verbal message. Don't interrupt with messages of your own. Occasionally nod, grunt or make non-committal responses (to encourage the teen to talk more). Do all the things you do naturally with your friends to show you're listening and you care. If you fail to do this, you deserve whatever happens to you!

SHARING 'N CARING -- THE PAYOFFS OF PAYING ATTENTION!

THE HIGH COST OF NOT LISTENING !!!

REFLECT! RELATE! -- a.k.a. REFLECTIVE LISTENING

Listening to and acknowledging your teen's feelings, experiences and point of view show respect and understanding, which is the foundation for problem solving. This is a skill that comes naturally to us when we relate to friends and other adults, so put your parental reflexes on hold. Listen with friendly ears, eyes, hearts and open minds.

Now for the fun part! As shown on page 74, the key is to tune in all your senses to what your teen is feeling and/or experiencing. Then, with genuineness and in a tentative way, show your teen you understand his message correctly. (Helpful hint: Teen actions speak louder than words, so focus on and relate to his feelings.)

Warning: **The Communication General has determined projecting your feelings and opinions into your listening responses is hazardous to your health and your teenager's.**

DOOR SLAMMER OR DOOR JAMMER?

If you don't listen and respond rationally in a respectful, caring, non-judgmental way, you train your teen not to come and talk to you about his life or problems! It can be aggravating or excruciating to hear your teen discussing things you don't want to hear, don't condone or can't control! But at least if he's talking to you about it, you aren't left in the dark. You're privy to what's going on. And you're still in a position to help him help himself or influence him in a positive direction (as warranted). That's a comforting tradeoff in itself!

So, think before you speak. Resist all initial impulses to help out, freak out, take over or take out! Bite your tongue, count to 100, put the muzzle back on—do whatever it takes to *keep the door open.*

TEEN TRANSMISSIONS	DOOR SLAMMERS!	DOOR JAMMERS!!

NOBODY LIKES ME! I'M FAT, I'M UGLY, I HAVE ZITS! I'M HOPELESS!!!

DON'T BE SILLY! EWE'S NOT FAT, EWE'S JUST FLUFFY!! I THINK YOU'RE CUTE AND CUDDLY, AND WONERFUL! IF OTHERS ARE TOO STUPID TO SEE THAT, THEN THAT'S *THEIR* PROBLEM!!

SOUNDS LIKE YOU'RE NOT FEELING VERY GOOD ABOUT YOURSELF...

YUCK!!... WE ALWAYS HAVE LEFTOVERS!!!

IS THIS THE KIND OF THANKS I GET FOR SCAVENGING ALL DAY?! MILLIONS ARE STARVING WHILE YOU SIT HERE COMPLAINING!! IF YOU DON'T LIKE IT, BUSTER, YOU CAN JUST BUZZ OFF!!!

YOU REALLY ARE FED UP WITH LEFTOVERS, HUH?! I SURE WISH I HAD SOMETHING FRESH FOR YOU...

I HATE GIRLS!! THEY'RE ALL A HERD OF PHONY PONIES!! I'M NEVER GETTING MARRIED!!!!

WHY BE STABLE?!

WHOA THERE, FELLA! YOU DON'T REALLY MEAN THAT!! I FELT THE SAME WAY AT YOUR AGE, BUT YOU'LL SEE, YOU'LL CHANGE YOUR MIND!!

OoooEEEE! SOUNDS LIKE YOU'VE HAD A RUN-IN WITH THE FILLIES?!!

TEEN TRANSMISSIONS

DOOR SLAMMERS!

DOOR JAMMERS !!

MOOOOOOO... I'VE GOT TWO EXAMS THIS WEEK, AN ESSAY, AND I'VE BEEN SCHEDULED TO DELIVER MILK EVERY MORNING!

OKAY, WHAT YOU SHOULD DO IS SET ASIDE A CERTAIN NUMBER OF HOURS EVERY DAY TO DO YOUR STUDIES! DON'T GO OUT, DON'T TALK ON THE PHONE AND NO T.V.! ALSO, YOU BETTER....

SOUNDS LIKE A BUSY WEEK!! -- HOW ARE YOU GOING TO SCHEDULE YOUR TIME?

BERRY BROKE UP WITH ME TO GO WITH GRIZELDA!...

sniffle...

BERRY'S A BOZO! I NEVER THOUGHT HE WAS RIGHT FOR YOU!! YOU'RE BETTER OFF WITHOUT HIM. JUST GRIN AND BEAR IT. YOU'LL GET OVER IT!

800000...

LOOKS LIKE YOU'RE REALLY HURTING... THAT MUST FEEL REALLY GRIZZLY!! IS THERE ANYTHING I CAN DO FOR YOU??...

8000000...

YOU'RE TREATING ME LIKE A KITTEN!! ALL MY FRIENDS GET TO STAY OUT LATER THAN I DO!!!

DON'T YOU DARE TALK TO ME IN THAT TONE OF VOICE!!! I DON'T CARE WHAT OTHERS ARE LETTING THEIR KIDS DO!! YOU'RE NOT OLD ENOUGH TO STAY OUT LATER UNTIL **I SAY SO**!!!!

MEOW! SOUNDS LIKE THIS IS A REALLY IMPORTANT ISSUE TO YOU!! LET'S SIT DOWN AND DISCUSS THIS AND SEE WHAT WE CAN COME UP WITH!!

80

TEEN TRANSMISSIONS | DOOR SLAMMERS! | DOOR JAMMERS!!

MOM?.. WHAT SHOULD A GIRL DO WHEN A GUY WANTS TO HAVE SEX? SOME GIRLS I KNOW HAVE ALREADY HAD SEX!!

WHAT??! YOU'RE TOO YOUNG TO BE THINKING ABOUT SUCH THINGS! SEX IS ONLY FOR MARRIED PEOPLE!! YOU BETTER NOT BE HORSING AROUND WITH BOYS!! I'LL TAN YORE HIDE!!!!

I'M SO GLAD YOU CAME TO ME WITH THIS QUESTION! I CAN GET YOU SOME BOOKS YOU'LL FIND VERY HELPFUL, THEN IF YOU STILL HAVE QUESTIONS WE CAN ALWAYS TALK ABOUT IT!

SCHOOL SUCKS! I WISH I'D NEVER FOLLOWED MARY THERE. MAYBE I SHOULD DROP OUT AND BECOME A BARBER?

YOU KNOW WHAT YOUR PROBLEM IS? YOU DON'T HAVE ANY SELF-DISCIPLINE!! YOU THINK EVERY-THING SHOULD BE HANDED TO YOU! I CAN SEE IT NOW, YOU'LL NEVER AMOUNT TO ANYTHING!!

...YES... SCHOOL IS DIFFICULT! BUT ARE YOU SURE DROPPING OUT IS WHAT YOU WANT TO DO??

GOSH! EVERYONE AT TABBI'S PARTY WAS GETTING STONED ON CATNIP LAST NIGHT!!

WHAT WERE YOU DOING AT A PARTY LIKE THAT, HUH? JUST FOR THAT YOU'RE GROUNDED FOR 2 WEEKS, AND I ORDER YOU TO STAY AWAY FROM TABBI, TOO! SISSSSS!!!

Hmmm.. AND HOW DID YOU FEEL ABOUT THAT??...

WHAT'S UP, DOC? --

If your teen is sending out non-verbal messages or you're unsure what he's feeling or why (or what he might be up to), or if he's simply not responding to your attempts to communicate, ask a non-prying (or clarifying) question. This helps convey you care and are trying to understand and you're here to help—not hassle! If your teen doesn't respond, don't force things. Ring back another time when he might be more receptive!

THE PURRFECT MODEL -- a.k.a. SHOW AND TELL

Guess who else has everyday trials, tribulations and feelings? You do! By sharing these with your teen, you are modeling (teaching) the art/skill of communicating experiences and feelings. This also helps him see and understand you as a real person. The way to stop feeling like an extraterrestrial is to stop acting like one.

PUTTING IT ALL TOGETHER...

Good listening skills are notorious for starting conversations. The peculiar thing about conversing (two-way communicating) is it usually enables people to find ways to solve their problems. If this is your goal or if you reluctantly find yourself in such a predicament, rely on all the skills in this book. (Note the Close-Encounters Checklist on page 86.) Memorize the following handy rule, and say your prayers.

CLOSE ENCOUNTERS COMMUNICATION SURVIVAL RULE:

ALWAYS HUMBLY SUM UP THE OTHER PERSON'S FEELINGS AND POSITION BEFORE STATING YOUR OWN (providing yours is necessary)!

85

☑ CLOSE-ENCOUNTERS CHECKLIST!! ☑

- ☑ Pick the right moment for both of you. Cool heads are best!
- ☑ Be conscious of your tone of voice, facial expressions, demeanor and body language.
- ☑ Don't overreact or underreact. (Good luck!)
- ☑ Don't accuse, insult or talk down to your teen. (Attack the problem.)
- ☑ Be friendly and fun or firm but kind. (No shouting or hitting.)
- ☑ Be open-minded, fair and honest. (Role model.)
- ☑ Focus on present situation and what needs to be done.
- ☑ State your feelings. (No whining. Skip the martyr routine.)
- ☑ Listen attentively, and get the facts.
- ☑ Acknowledge teen's feelings, experiences and point of view.
- ☑ Extend respect, understanding, trust, encouragement, responsibility and love.
- ☑ Don't try to control or win. (Give and take and negotiate.)
- ☑ Arrive at a solution (before you-know-what freezes over).
- ☑ Rest up for next encounter!

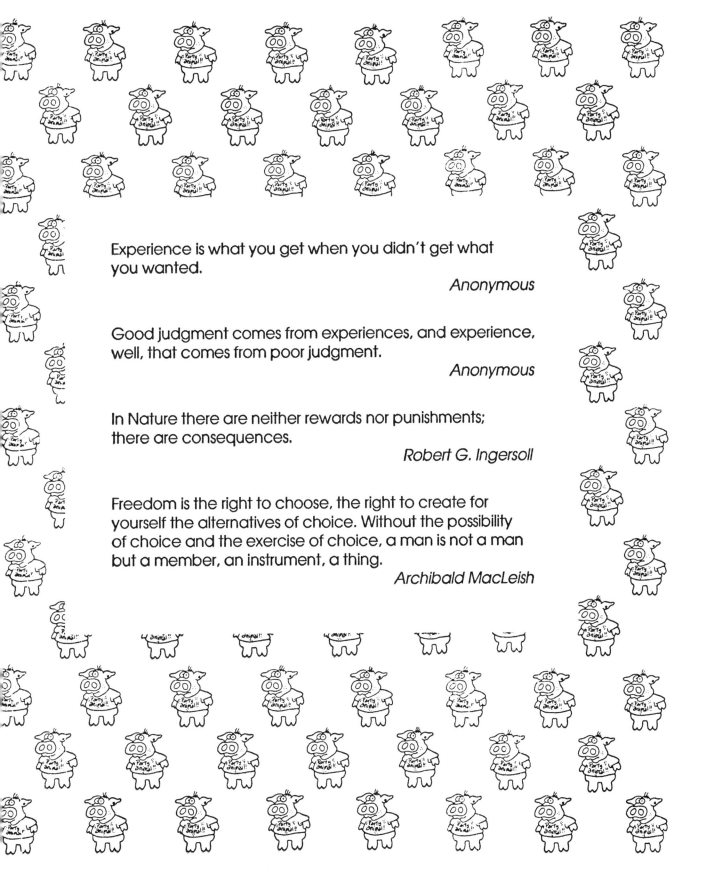

Experience is what you get when you didn't get what you wanted.

Anonymous

Good judgment comes from experiences, and experience, well, that comes from poor judgment.

Anonymous

In Nature there are neither rewards nor punishments; there are consequences.

Robert G. Ingersoll

Freedom is the right to choose, the right to create for yourself the alternatives of choice. Without the possibility of choice and the exercise of choice, a man is not a man but a member, an instrument, a thing.

Archibald MacLeish

BLUEPRINT FOR CHANGE

A SIMPLE HOW-TO FOR THE CONSTRUCTION OF A "SELF-REGULATING" SYSTEM FOR MANAGING TEEN BEHAVIOR -- (no foolin'!).

STRUCTURAL OBJECTIVES:

To progressively allow maturing teenager to assume responsibility for running his own life.

To establish mutual respect, trust and harmony for the sake of sanity and survival of all family members.

CONSTRUCTION DETAILS:

Responsibilities, expectations (rules, chores, conduct) and any consequences are discussed/negotiated with teen in advance or as each new situation arises. (Teen is more cooperative and less likely to misbehave or rebel if he is allowed to negotiate matters that concern his life.)

Parents: Let go, extend trust and respect, provide encouragement and consistently ensure teen be allowed to experience (learn from) the consequences of his/her behavior.

LOGISTICS:

➡ Teen and parents know teen has control of his own fate. Teen can improve his situation or make it worse, but it's his choice and responsibility.

➡ Teenager becomes more responsible, experiences increased self-esteem, gains confidence and respects/appreciates parents more. Teen also misbehaves a lot less (fewer *reasons* to rebel).

THE MASTER PLAN

SITUATIONS, RESPONSIBILITIES, RULES AND ANY POSSIBLE CONSEQUENCES ARE DISCUSSED, NEGOTIATED AND UNDERSTOOD. ENCOURAGEMENT AND TRUST ARE EXTENDED.

RIGHT/GOOD/DECENT APPROPRIATE BEHAVIOR

WRONG/BAD/STUPID INAPPROPRIATE BEHAVIOR

TEENAGER'S CHOICE!!

POSITIVE CONSEQUENCES ENCOURAGEMENT/PRAISE

NEGATIVE CONSEQUENCES DISINVOLVEMENT

NOTE: POSITIVE AND NEGATIVE CONSEQUENCES, ENCOURAGEMENT AND PRAISE, AND DISINVOLVEMENT ARE DISCUSSED IN DETAIL IN THE SECTIONS THAT FOLLOW.

THE SPONTANEOUS MASTER PLAN

Analyze situation.

Determine who owns problem.

Take appropriate action or inaction (be consistent).

If situation warrants parental involvement, use good communication skills to explain what you expect or need of your teen. Point out what the consequences are (when necessary). Be fair and open to negotiation as warranted, but keep the focus on the immediate situation.

 **Future hassle-preventer and timesaver—**Make sure you and your teenager understand the same expectations and consequences automatically apply to any such future situations as well.

 **Novices and neurotics take note!** Not all situations warrant rules and/or negotiations or explaining the consequences! It's OK to respectfully and kindly state the facts, and expect the teen's cooperation. (No cooperation? Read on.)

YOU UNLOCK THIS DOOR WITH THE KEY OF COMMUNICATION. BEYOND IT IS ANOTHER DIMENSION... A DIMENSION OF SOUND... A DIMENSION OF SIGHT... A DIMENSION OF MIND... YOU'RE MOVING INTO AN IMPROVED RELATIONSHIP OF BOTH SHADOW AND SUBSTANCE... OF THINGS AND IDEAS... YOU'VE JUST CROSSED OVER INTO...

The CONSEQUENCE ZONE

CONSEQUENCES-- THE RIGHT STUFF

Reality—*The consequences/results of any behavior; the enlightening process by which experience is acquired.*

Consequences, positive or negative, are the most important tools you have to change teen behavior and for instilling responsibility. Reality will make a greater impression on your teen than your amateurish (serious) impersonation of either Rambo or Mother Teresa. Some consequences occur naturally, while others will have to be custom designed to fit the crime and/or the personality of the perpetrator. At every conceivable opportunity, you must *consistently* allow your teen to experience whatever consequences naturally or logically follow his behavior, good or bad (within reason, of course).

Don't forget—Wean the teen on low-risk consequences first, working up to the heavy stuff before age 18.

NATURAL CONSEQUENCES -- *100% NATURAL; CONTAINS NO PARENTAL ADDITIVES!*

These consequences occur naturally, without any assistance or contrivance on your part. Time, hunger, discomfort, embarrassment, happiness/unhappiness and other consequences are the natural by-products of teen behavior, as are natural social consequences (ones that occur outside your jurisdiction). For natural consequences to be effective, you must stand back and let Mother Nature and society do their thing!

SITUATION	NATURAL CONSEQUENCES

Doesn't set alarm.	*Oversleeps, is late for school, gets tardy slip.*

Doesn't study.	*Fails course, is dropped from team.*

94

Is late for dinner.
Food is cold or all gone.

Doesn't take care of clothes.
No clean clothes to wear.

Exceeds speed limit.
If caught, pays fine himself.

Overdue library book.
Must pay charges himself.

LOGICAL CONSEQUENCES-- *LENDING MOTHER NATURE A HELPING HAND.*

These consequences require some assistance on your part. The teen needs to be able to see the *direct association* between his behavior and the ensuing, logical result/consequence—be it positive or negative! If the consequence isn't logically related to his behavior, he won't get the right message. (Also see Encouragement, pages 106 to 108, and Disinvolvement, pages 110 to 112.)

CREATIVE POSITIVE CONSEQUENCES-- THE "CARE" NECESSITIES!

Encouragement and praise (see pages 106 to 108) are excellent primary positive consequences to use for your teen. You may occasionally want to do something special to show him you're proud of him, that you love him or are thinking of him. You need to be a role model for thoughtfulness, recognition, appreciation and spontaneous generosity!

(**Rule:** Do not "treat" an existing behavior. Reserve treats for something new, special or out of the ordinary. The teen should never expect it.)

CREATIVE NEGATIVE CONSEQUENCES-- THE "BEAR" NECESSITIES!

On extremely rare occasions, you'll have no choice but to create a fair and reasonable negative consequence to get some point across (no TV, no phone, no BMW). Whenever possible, try calmly and respectfully to ask the teen what he thinks a fair or appropriate consequence (punishment*) should be in a given situation. He's more likely to be reasonable and cooperative if he's had a say in his fate. Even criminals get to plea bargain!

*Punishment is any negative consequence—natural or logical. In fact, natural and logical consequences are often their own best (or worst) punishment. Artificially contrived (creative) negative consequences often run the risk of evoking resentment and rebellion.

CREATIVE NEGATIVE CONSEQUENCES PERMIT

OFFICIALLY AUTHORIZED PERMIT TO BE USED IN CASE OF AN EMERGENCY ONLY!!!

BEING OF ALLEGEDLY SOUND MIND, I HEREBY AGREE WHEN ALL NATURAL AND LOGICAL CONSEQUENCES HAVE BEEN EXHAUSTED, AND/OR ARE NON-EXISTENT-- AND ONLY WHEN WARRANTED AND AT MY OWN RISK-- I WILL BE PERMITTED TO CREATE (AND/OR NEGOTIATE) AN APPROPRIATE CONSEQUENCE. I FURTHER AGREE TO USE MY BEST EFFORTS AND/OR COMMON SENSE TO ENSURE THE CONSEQUENCE SHALL FAIRLY FIT THE CRIME AND BE APPROPRIATELY CUSTOMIZED TO THE UNIQUE PERSONALITY OF THE PERPETRATOR. I AM AWARE IF THE CONSEQUENCE IS NOT APPROPRIATE, IT WILL NOT CHANGE THE BEHAVIOR AND MAY RESULT IN "NEGATIVE CONSEQUENCES" FOR MYSELF.

SIGNED_____ DATE_____

DOCTOR _____ INSURANCE COMPANY_____

NEXT OF KIN_____

OFFICIAL

WITNESS _____

AUTHORIZED BY _____

103

WHEN THE GOING GETS TOUGH...

When a consequence isn't working, re-evaluate and renegotiate. With some ingenuity and flexibility, you and your teen may agree on backup consequences for the original consequence, trading chores/favors or other plans of action that work for you. Implementing changes takes time and requires patience and consistent follow-through on your part.

Most teens will negotiate and cooperate when you appeal to their sensibilities and sense of fair play. You need to remember to treat your teen with dignity and respect, and let him have a say in his own consequences!

If your teen is unusually uncooperative, it may be an indication of an "underlying cause." Your teen may view some consequences as punishment. This usually happens when you apply a consequence in anger or in an unpleasant tone of voice. Getting emotional or trying to force the situation only makes matters worse. *The foundation for cooperation lies in developing an open, communicative, respectful, loving relationship with your teen.*

Another underlying cause might be an undisclosed grievance. Your teen may be seeking revenge, struggling for control of his own life or testing limits by doing something he knows will bother you. For example, if your teen feels you're treating him like a baby, he might start ignoring curfew as a way to make a stand. The real issue isn't really how late he stays out, but how he's being treated in general. In an open-minded, level-headed, *respectful* way, talk with him and listen. This should help you find the underlying cause (real issue).

While it's OK for parents to have realistic, non-negotiable limits, you may discover you need to compromise on some issues more than you'd like. At other times, you may be unable to reach an agreement at all. When you encounter unmanageable behaviors and/or can't reach an agreement, it might be wise to see a family counselor. Emotions, objectivity and communication-clarification issues are all mitigating factors. Or there could be deeper issues, such as substance abuse, emotional problems or psychotic disturbances.

The human mind is infinitely complex—it's comforting to know there are trained professionals to help you with your emotional needs just as there are professionals for your automotive, financial and medical needs. Most professionals base their fees on a sliding scale and have flexible hours. Check with your doctor, pastor or friends for a reference. Or consult the Yellow Pages for referrals or listings.

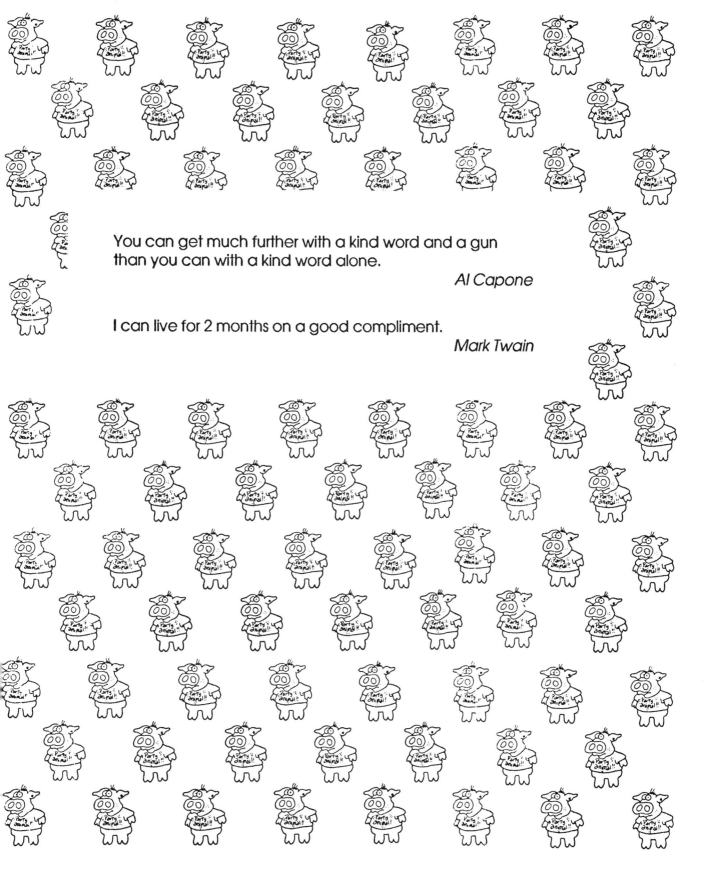

You can get much further with a kind word and a gun than you can with a kind word alone.

Al Capone

I can live for 2 months on a good compliment.

Mark Twain

Home... home on the range...
Where the TEENS and the PARENTS all play...
Where SELDOM is HEARD
An ENCOURAGING WORD...
And the skies there are CLOUDY ALL DAY!!

...sniffle

I'd yodel but I'm a LITTLE HORSE...

ENCOURAGEMENT and PRAISE

If your teen hasn't measured up to your expectations, his own expectations or what he perceives as society's expectations of him, he's probably a very discouraged, underachieving sideliner by now. Having lost confidence in himself, he ceases to tackle any positive activities in which he might excel. This makes others see him as a hopeless fumbler, too. In frustration, he may turn to spoilsport activities where he's sure to get on the (wrong) scoreboard. He behaves like a loser because he's convinced he is a loser.

106

Even an incorrigible teen is an "encourageable" teen. Encouragement and praise can transform most losers into winners (and get your relationship back on track). *You need* to pay more attention to the teen's positive behaviors and assets than to his screw ups and liabilities. How can you tackle this tricky play? Parents describe their proven maneuvers.

A word to the wise—Encouragements can be perceived as unrealistic expectations if you're insensitive to your teen's needs, abilities and interests. And you know what that can mean!

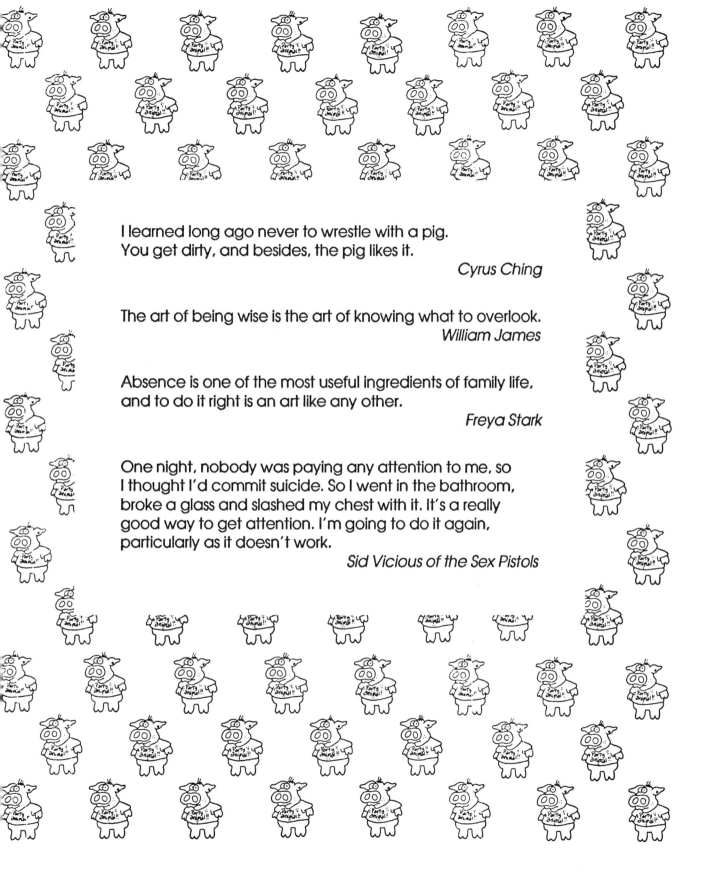

I learned long ago never to wrestle with a pig.
You get dirty, and besides, the pig likes it.

Cyrus Ching

The art of being wise is the art of knowing what to overlook.

William James

Absence is one of the most useful ingredients of family life,
and to do it right is an art like any other.

Freya Stark

One night, nobody was paying any attention to me, so
I thought I'd commit suicide. So I went in the bathroom,
broke a glass and slashed my chest with it. It's a really
good way to get attention. I'm going to do it again,
particularly as it doesn't work.

Sid Vicious of the Sex Pistols

DISINVOLVEMENT -- a.k.a. IGNORING, WITHDRAWAL

WHAT IF THEY GAVE A WAR AND NOBODY CAME?

How can anyone fight, or continue fighting, if the other team won't even take the field or the other team leaves? Not getting involved is a powerful tactic when the teen is misbehaving strictly to manipulate you (power struggles, arguing, fighting, acting helpless). In these situations, your involvement (no matter how good your intentions) only *reinforces* the misbehavior and/or *escalates* the conflict.

STEPS TO TAKE TO AVOID GETTING SUCKED OR SUCKERED INTO NEEDLESS CONFLICTS:

 ① Don't respond emotionally. (No anger, guilt, pity, fear.)

② Communicate understanding and concern/care. Show willingness to discuss issues later when everyone is calm (and unarmed).

③ Withdraw physically, leave the room, leave the house, leave! Or hold your ground, but pretend the teen is no longer there. (Feel free to hum or sing the Stones' song "I Can't Get No Satisfaction." This will help drown out the annoying sounds of begging, nagging and arguing!)

④ Let other consequences—natural or logical—take over. (Note: It's considered rude to smile or laugh.)

TO ENGAGE OR NOT TO ENGAGE; THAT IS THE QUESTION

DISINVOLVEMENT HAS ITS PLACE. BUT DON'T GO OVERBOARD AND WITHDRAW FROM YOUR TEEN WHEN HE REALLY **NEEDS** YOU. DON'T IGNORE BEHAVIORS THAT ARE DISRUPTIVE OR HARMFUL OR ONES THAT ARE ACTUALLY A SERIOUS CALL FOR HELP (LIKE DEPRESSION)! BE WISE, ANALYZE AND USE YOUR PARENTAL RADAR!!

Remember—By consistently paying more attention to the teen when he's not misbehaving, you lovingly show him attention and self-worth are obtainable through positive behaviors and fair play—not through shallow manipulations. As a bonus, this will eliminate many misbehaviors that existed merely because of the teen's misdirected "need" for your attention.

SAY, SON! HOW ABOUT US GOING AND GETTING SOME GRAVY TRAIN, AND THEN SEE <u>CATS</u> ON BROADWAY?

Well... I WAS going to go chase cars with the pack, maybe 'borrow' a few hubcaps... but, sure! Why NOT? It might be fun. Dad's not such a bad dude!...

O.K.!

I ♥ cars!

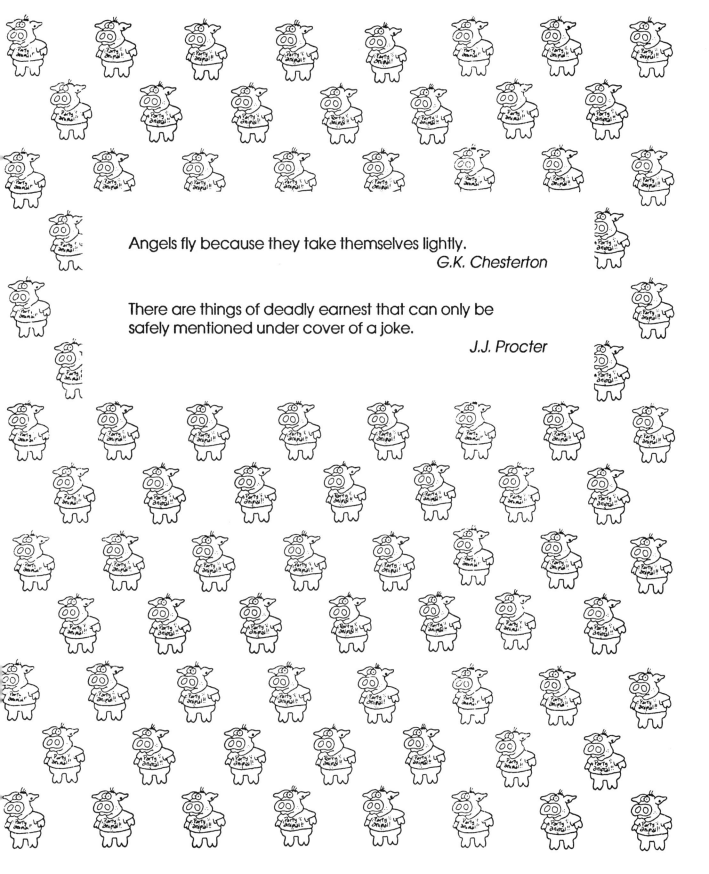

Angels fly because they take themselves lightly.

G.K. Chesterton

There are things of deadly earnest that can only be
safely mentioned under cover of a joke.

J.J. Procter

COMIC RELIEF -- THE PARENT THAT LAUGHS, LASTS!

MOTTOES:

THE FAMILY THAT PLAY'S TOGETHER STAY'S TOGETHER.

IT'S EASIER TO RECOVER FROM A BAD JOKE THAN A BAD ARGUMENT.

If you haven't got a sense of humor, you're advised to beg, borrow, rent or steal one. A parent without a sense of humor is like french fries without salt, catsup, double-beef cheeseburger or chocolate shake. A humorless parent stands as much chance as a snowball in the Sahara. All teens have a sense of humor. (Think yours doesn't? What about the last time he laughed in your face or behind your back?!) Humor brings out the kid in you and enables you to say the nastiest thing in a funny way. (A spoonful of sugar helps the medicine go down!) Best of all, humor lets you speak a common language with your teen.

THE BUSINESS-AS-USUAL APPROACH (yawn)

AN ENTERTAINING ALTERNATIVE

The following are some ways to make fun not war. Improvisations allowed. Make sure your teen knows you're trying to be funny. Make sure you smile or laugh after you deliver your performance. (Corny jokes and puns are used at your own risk. Too many of any one type of joke or comic send up can be a turn-off.)

BASIC -- SMILE A LOT!! It may make your teen wonder what you're up to, but it also makes you look happy, friendly, in a good mood and very approachable. (Same is true for whistling, humming and singing.)

WHISTLE, HUM OR SING your favorite tune or one that coincidentally (strategically) relates to your feelings or an issue. ("I Can't Get No Satisfaction," "Help") Do a parody of some songs and substitute different words or phrases.

TELL AND SHARE JOKES. Ask your teen if he's heard any good ones. There are plenty of joke books available that will make you lethal in this department. (Save the X-rated ones for your X-rated friends. Your teen has probably already heard them anyway.)

DO CHARACTER IMPERSONATIONS OF COMEDIANS OR PERSONALITIES! Have PeeWee Herman or Steve Martin tell your teen what to do. Another time let Rambo or Dirty Harry do your dirty work. This can be a blast for you and your teen.

DO LINES AND CHARACTERS FROM FAVORITE T.V. SHOWS OR MOVIES! Impersonate the actor and deliver the line. Do everyone from Cosby and Bogart to Boris Karloff and Mary Poppins. Do a takeoff from *Saturday Night Live* and other shows. (And they said TV was bad for you!) This works for everything from horror films to musicals. Say it or sing it.

WISECRACKS, COMEBACKS AND PUNS are for those with sharp minds. Lay a "mind field" for your teen. (If God didn't mean for people like us to do this, He wouldn't have created people who set themselves up for it!) Wisecracks can be callous or insulting if not handled with tact. And be prepared to take it if you dish it out. Puns are considered the lowest form of humor. But so what? Gopher it!

ALTER YOUR TONE OF VOICE AND MANNERISMS! Fake an accent (foreign or domestic). Or try raising or lowering the pitch of your voice to make yourself sound weird or playful. Imitate a sportscaster and give a narrative (great for sibling rivalry). Say "No" to nagging teens by hissing and howling like a cat or growling and barking like a mad dog. (It's fun, and it works!)

BE MELODRAMATIC! When your teen offends or hurts you, clutch your heart and overdramatize having a heart attack. Or act like you've been stabbed in the heart, and pretend to pull the knife out. The tantrum is also a goodie! Talk in a loud, nasal whine, pout and stomp your foot for emphasis.

FOR A SPITTING IMAGE keep up on teen vocabulary, inside jokes and gestures. It's OK to have fun by borrowing their catch phrases and words—occasionally. (Acting or dressing their age for real is a major turn off.)

PLAY SAFE AND FUN PRANKS OR PRACTICAL JOKES! Hide behind the door when your teen comes home past curfew, and jump out. (Serves him right.) When he's not looking, eat some of his dinner. Put his (clean) underwear on your head while folding the laundry, saying you found a new hat! Threaten to tickle him to pieces if he doesn't cooperate.

Humor is not right for all situations, but it can come in very handy and has been known to diffuse many potentially explosive situations. It's hard to argue with someone who is making you laugh. Why fight if you can have fun?

RED ALERT!!--

Anger can masquerade as humor in the form of sarcasm. This is passive-aggressive behavior—not authentic humor. The telltale sign: making innocent, funny zingers (cutting remarks) about something you're really bothered or angry about and following it up with, "I'm sorry. I was only kidding." (Were you, really?) Use good communication skills to express anger appropriately.

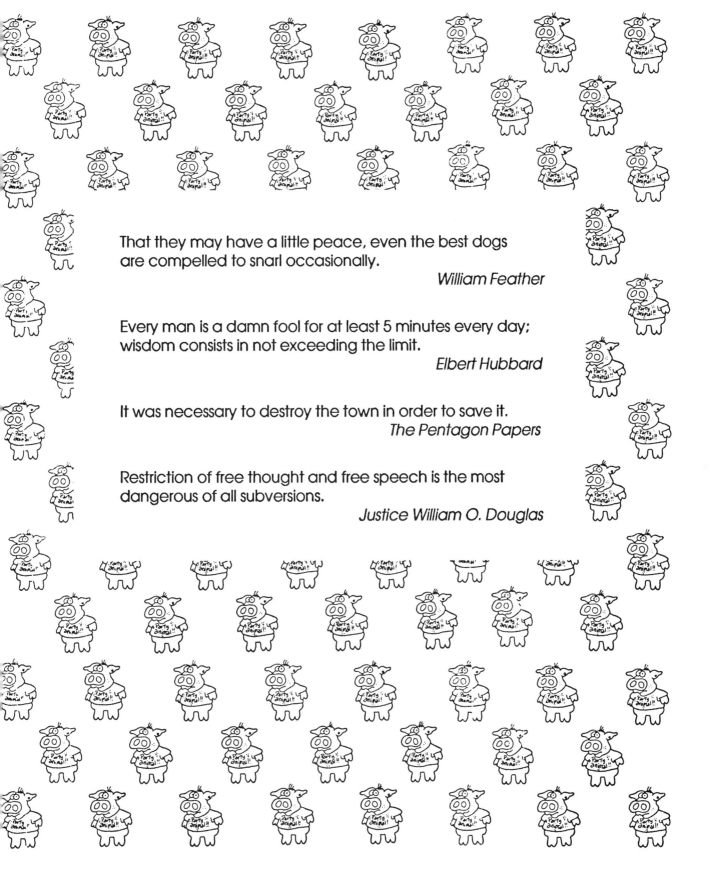

That they may have a little peace, even the best dogs
are compelled to snarl occasionally.

William Feather

Every man is a damn fool for at least 5 minutes every day;
wisdom consists in not exceeding the limit.

Elbert Hubbard

It was necessary to destroy the town in order to save it.

The Pentagon Papers

Restriction of free thought and free speech is the most
dangerous of all subversions.

Justice William O. Douglas

SPONTANEOUS SPARRING SPATS-- a.k.a. FIGHTING, CONFLICT, WWIII

DIPLOMACY--THE ART OF SAYING "NICE DOGGIE" TILL
YOU CAN FIND A ROCK. -- Wynn Catlin

Despite all the improved parenting skills, love, understanding, money and lavish gifts, you're still going to be ambushed by sudden emotions and situations that must be dealt with immediately, whether sitting down, standing up or from midair. It's an unavoidable, natural occurrence that takes place between all individuals who are different or who come from different planets.

Fights needn't be destructive, no-win clashes. They can be handled constructively and are actually an important *safety valve* in a healthy relationship. It helps if the opponents understand the purpose of any spat is to courteously communicate needs and feelings and arrive at a solution or compromise (if possible), in spite of the emotionally charged atmosphere. It also helps if aspirin is on hand and there are no lethal weapons within easy reach of either opponent.

Hmmm... I HEAR WHAT YOU'RE SAYING. I CAN SEE HOW FRUSTRATING THIS MUST BE FOR YOU. OK THEN, LET'S DISCUSS IT AND SEE IF WE CAN'T COME UP WITH A FAIR SOLUTION!

HA! WHAT'S _FAIR_ ABOUT ANY CURFEW?!!

WELL, A CURFEW HELPS YOU LEARN HOW TO MANAGE YOUR TIME AND YOUR SOCIAL LIFE, AND HOW TO BE DEPENDABLE. IT ALSO HELPS US MONITOR YOUR SAFETY -- WE CARE ABOUT YOU TOO MUCH FOR YOU TO BE OUT AT ALL HOURS OR BE TOO SLEEPY TO DO WELL IN SCHOOL! SO... WHAT WOULD YOU SAY TO A LATER, BASIC CURFEW AND MAYBE A FLEXIBLE ONE FOR SPECIAL SITUATIONS?

YEAH, 'CAUSE SOME THINGS DON'T EVEN _START_ UNTIL PRETTY LATE OR ARE SO FAR AWAY!!

OK, HOW ABOUT WE SAY NINE-THIRTY FOR WEEK NIGHTS AND MIDNIGHT FOR WEEKENDS? AND WE CAN DISCUSS THE TIME FOR SPECIAL SITUATIONS AS THEY ARISE. BUT-- I WANT YOU TO ALWAYS CALL IF YOU'RE GOING TO BE LATE, OK?!

OK. I GUESS THAT'S FAIR.

123

FEELINGS

Anger—Grrrrrrr! Anger is an essential, healthy part of communicating. You can't beat it for its surefire way of letting someone know you're upset or you really mean business or for blowing off steam. It's normal and healthy to be angry with your teenager. Your disapproval shows necessary concern and love. And it's normal and healthy for your teenager to be angry with you, too!

THE ADVANTAGES OF ALLOWING YOUR TEEN HIS FREEDOM OF FAIR EXPRESSION

- It shows mutual respect.
- The lines of communication stay open.
- Resolutions are faster, which eliminates the need for rebellious counterattacks because he's gotten it out of his system by letting off steam. Everyone feels better sooner.
- He learns how to deal with his emotions.
- He'll stop spray painting nasty graffiti about you all over town.
- It's the precursor to free speech in the "real" (free) world.

A successful spat depends on you being a role model for communication skills and making sure everyone adheres to the "Rules of the Ring." Sometimes your teen will be right and you'll be wrong. Don't be a role model for how to be a dipstick, OK? Own up to your humanity—you'll never be sorry you said you were sorry.

RULES OF THE RING

(COMPILED BY PROFESSIONAL REFEREE DON JOHNSON, Ph.D.)*

THE WHITE GLOVE MOTTO -- ATTACK THE PROBLEM NOT EACH OTHER!

FAIR FIGHTING

Only one person talks at a time
Express thoughts and feelings
Be assertive and direct
Use "I" sentences
Listen to each other
Be open-minded
Talk about *present* conflict
Respect confidentiality
Don't try to win
Finish the fight or agree
   to postpone it
Listen actively
Reflect feelings

DIRTY FIGHTING

More than one person talking
Yelling or screaming
Abuse—physical and/or verbal,
   name calling, put-downs,
   hitting, cursing
Blaming, accusing, threats
Bringing up the past
Leaving or avoiding
Closing up (not talking)
Ganging up (2 against 1)
Blackmailing
Mind reading (knowing what
   another is thinking/feeling)
Scapegoating (not my fault)
Trying to win

*Adolescent psychotherapist

ARF FINKLETTER HERE!! It's time for another edition of "Parents Say the DARNDEST THINGS"!!! Now... let's listen to some darn things parents from our studio audience say to their teenagers!!...

WHEN I WAS YOUR AGE...

I'M *ONLY* DOING THIS FOR *YOUR* OWN *GOOD*! SOMEDAY YOU'LL *THANK ME*!!!...

IF ALL YOUR FRIENDS HOPPED OFF A CLIFF, WOULD *YOU* HOP, TOO??

WHERE WERE YOU WHEN THEY PASSED OUT THE BRAINS??!

THIS HURTS *ME* MORE THAN IT HURTS YOU!!...

DO YOU THINK MONEY GROWS ON *TREES*??..

STOP ACTING LIKE A BABY!!!

WAIT TILL YOU'RE OLDER, YOU'LL UNDERSTAND...

I CAN'T WAIT TILL YOU GROW UP AND HAVE A KID JUST LIKE *YOU*!!!

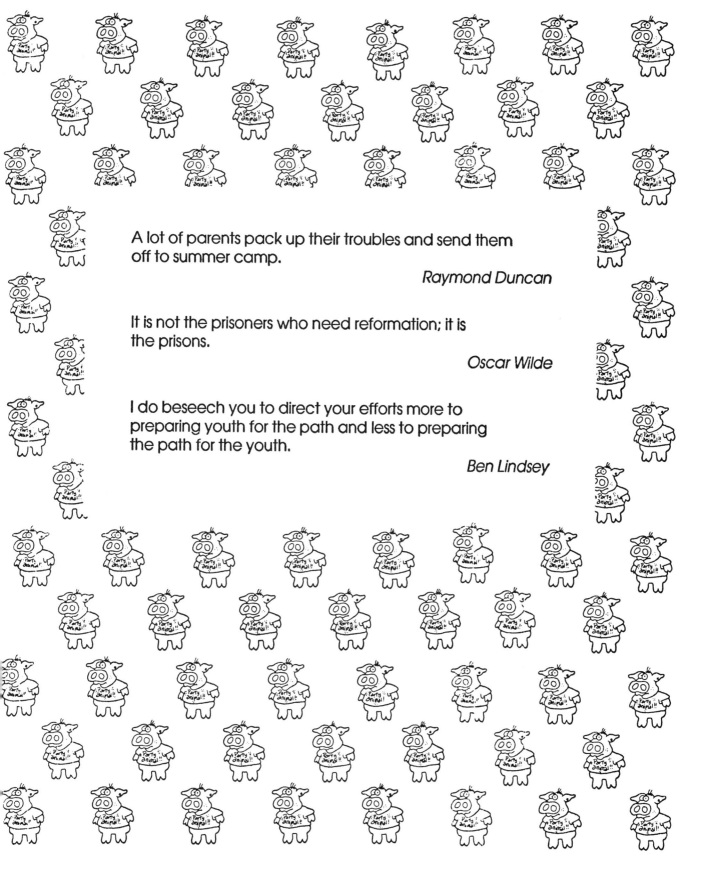

A lot of parents pack up their troubles and send them off to summer camp.

Raymond Duncan

It is not the prisoners who need reformation; it is the prisons.

Oscar Wilde

I do beseech you to direct your efforts more to preparing youth for the path and less to preparing the path for the youth.

Ben Lindsey

HASSLEFREE HOMES --a.k.a. ENVIRONMENTAL MODIFICATION; PREVENTIVE DISCIPLINE

DOES THIS SOUND FAMILIAR?...

SORRY I'M HOME *LATE*; I GOT *LOST*!

I THOUGHT YOU SAID *YOU* WERE GOING TO CANCEL MY VET APPOINTMENT!!

MOM? I'M AT THE NEIGHBOR'S HOUSE. I FORGOT MY KEYS, AND I'M *LOCKED* OUT!! CAN YOU COME HOME AND LET ME IN?...I *NEED* MY BALLET SHOES!!!

OH!...I FORGOT TO TELL YOU BUT A MR. FISHER CALLED *LAST NIGHT* AND SAID FOR YOU TO CALL *HIM*, THAT IT WAS *URGENT*!!

Tired of trying to talk or lecture your teen into responsible behavior?
Want to prevent some unnecessary hassles in your castle?

Take heart. Invaluable natural environmental resources abound. Harvesting these natural resources and combining them with the techniques in this book will make you a lean-keen-parent-machine. Part of your duty is to train and prepare your teen for environmental self-sufficiency. What better way than to get on-the-job training from a 100% natural, caring pro like you!

— An ounce of prevention is worth a pound of cure!!
......

ENVIRONMENTAL RESOURCES-- TAKING SOME HASSLE OUT OF THE CASTLE

A TEENAGER SHOULD HAVE HIS/HER OWN:

CALENDAR--

To use for scheduling appointments, events, chores, wild parties, remembering parents' birthdays.

WRISTWATCH AND ALARM CLOCK--

He can tell time, and he knows what time he needs to be places, wake up for school, etc. If God wanted you to be a timepiece, you'd have a buzzer where your mouth is.

SPENDING MONEY (ALLOWANCE)--

Give him money weekly or bimonthly. Let him learn how to budget it. Avoid loans. Agree on what your teen is not expected to purchase with his own money (school lunches, books). Insist on a spare emergency quarter for phone calls. Teach him how to write checks and balance a checkbook. Have mature teens open own checking account—super prep for college life!

HOUSE KEYS/CAR KEYS--

No hassles with borrowing or losing your keys. No more excuses for getting locked out of the house. You can always change the locks when he turns 18.

AUTOMOBILE (OPTIONAL)--

No more hassles over sharing the family car or worrying about your car getting wrecked. Negotiate who pays for the car, gas and insurance. Agree on mobility restrictions, limitations, freedoms. You can always let the air out of the tires or take away the keys as needed (the *ultimate* negative consequence).

DRIVER'S PREP--

Teach your teen the way around town and how to read a map. He should know the location of hospitals, minor emergency centers, doctors' offices, stores, banks and other places he may need to go. No "I got lost" excuses! Insist he keep an updated city map (and personal telephone directory) in the car at all times. Every teen (boys and girls) should also know how to change a flat tire, when to call a tow truck and so forth.

RADIO/"JAM BOX"/STEREO--

For listening and playing their music and for hearing weather reports to ascertain their clothing ensemble for the day. Headphones are a must, at any price.

PERSONAL SPACE --

Bedroom, closet space, shelves, storage items. Allow privacy on the phone or in bedroom. Knock before entering—show some respect! Dark basements or dungeons a possibility for extreme cases.

BIOAWARENESS--

Does caffeine affect him? Does too much sugar? Any food allergies? PMS? Low blood sugar? Too little sleep? Too much alcohol? Special medication needs? Encourage teen to become aware of, and responsible for, his body's needs. Preventable, adverse side effects of physical conditions don't justify hassling others. For example, side effects of low blood sugar (hypoglycemia) are fatigue, depression, wild mood swings and psychotic behavior. You may be battling a substance or disease, not just a teenager! When in doubt, check it out.

A TEENAGER SHOULD BE ENCOURAGED TO:

MAKE AND KEEP HIS OWN APPOINTMENTS--

Babysitting, doctor, dentist. If he's old enough to drive, let him drive to the appointment. Give him a check or money to take, if necessary. Meanwhile, you can enjoy yourself. When you're at an appointment with him, let *him* fill out forms, answer questions, etc.

TAKE PHONE MESSAGES--

Explain how you want phone messages taken the first time, then expect it.

SHARE IN FAMILY PLANS--

Discuss trips and activities to solicit teen's input. Try not to laugh.

SHARE IN PLANNING AND EXECUTION OF CHORES--

Discuss chores, negotiate fairly and get cooperation. No freeloaders, and no training him to be a freeloader.

DO OWN PERSONAL SERVICES
(FLEXIBLE; VARIES WITH AGE) --

Let him fend for himself in the kitchen (cook and clean), do own laundry, keep up with personal belongings, go to the store, run errands. Explain how-to for first-time events, such as laundry, preparing meals, using appliances. Look for opportunities to train him for independence, not dependence.

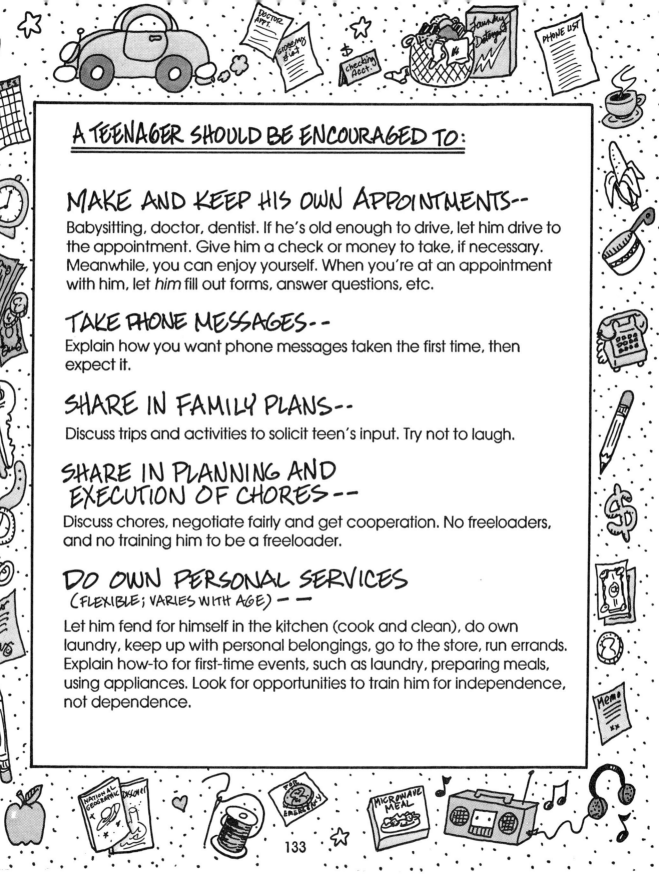

FAMILY MEMO BOARDS--

Chalk or cork for posting phone messages, leaving notes for each other, recording appointments, drawing silly pictures.

POSTED PHONE LIST--

Make thorough list with numbers for doctor, dentist, stores, friends, police, ambulance. Keep it next to phone(s) for convenience or emergency.

CALL-WAITING PHONE SERVICE--

This lets talkative teen or anyone else know when there's an incoming call. A second phone line or teen's private line (with answering machine other than parents') is a luxurious option.

NEWSPAPER/MAGAZINES --

These are great for looking up weather reports, reference material for school and enriching inquiring minds. A good set of encyclopedias is commendable, too.

SPARE HOUSE KEY --

Hide an extra key somewhere outside. Even parents lose keys and lock themselves out or forget keys occasionally. Make a rule to put the key back immediately after use, or you'll all be sorry!

CONVENIENCE FOODS--

Too tired or busy to cook? Not home? Keep healthy foodstuffs in the pantry or freezer for teen to prepare for himself or the family as a matter of necessity or for convenience. Solicit input for stocking up. Encourage your teen to learn how to cook simple foods or meals. It's great "real-world" training. (Keep plenty of antacid on hand.)

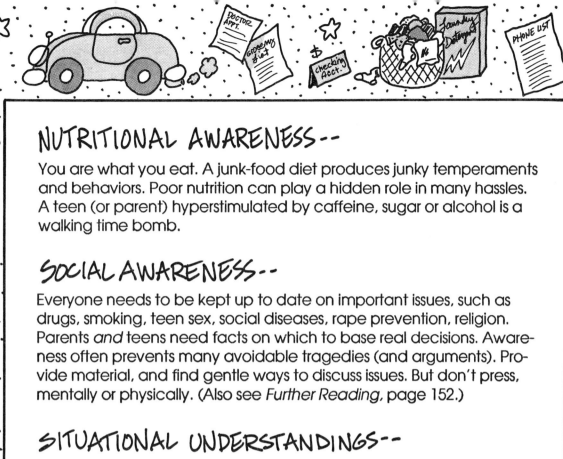

NUTRITIONAL AWARENESS--

You are what you eat. A junk-food diet produces junky temperaments and behaviors. Poor nutrition can play a hidden role in many hassles. A teen (or parent) hyperstimulated by caffeine, sugar or alcohol is a walking time bomb.

SOCIAL AWARENESS--

Everyone needs to be kept up to date on important issues, such as drugs, smoking, teen sex, social diseases, rape prevention, religion. Parents *and* teens need facts on which to base real decisions. Awareness often prevents many avoidable tragedies (and arguments). Provide material, and find gentle ways to discuss issues. But don't press, mentally or physically. (Also see *Further Reading*, page 152.)

SITUATIONAL UNDERSTANDINGS--

Get a mutual verbal understanding beforehand of each other's expectations and responsibilities in any situation, such as when asked to pick up your teen from somewhere (the mall). Agree on precise location, time, etc. Make sure your teen knows the address of any new destination in advance (have a map in your car for backup). The more you spell out details in advance and "synchronize your watches," the fewer misunderstandings (and nervous breakdowns) there will be.

WHAT OTHER THINGS CAN YOU THINK OF??--

Everyone is different. Adapt your environment to fully meet your family's needs. Get input from all family members. When adapting the environment, *don't do anything for another person he can and should do for himself.*

HARVESTING ENVIRONMENTAL RESOURCES

When a new hassle comes up, ask yourself if there is anything you can change in the environment to eliminate the problem in the future, then change it. (Also see the Spontaneous Master Plan, page 90). Hasslefree parents are a key part of the teen environment. Smart parents don't want to have to be involved any more than absolutely necessary, so the more you can harness environmental resources, the easier your job will be!

It's fun and challenging to train your teen for self-sufficiency and know he's realistically prepared to take care of himself when he leaves home. It's the greatest gift you can give him—and yourself!

YOU KNOW, MOM, I USED TO THINK YOU WERE SO MEAN TO MAKE ME LEARN HOW TO COOK, CLEAN, DO LAUNDRY, MAKE APPOINTMENTS, BUDGET MONEY, ETC.!! BUT MOST OF MY FRIENDS AT COLLEGE NEVER HAD TO DO ANYTHING! YOU SHOULD SEE THEM, THEY'RE A MESS!! IT'S REALLY SAD!

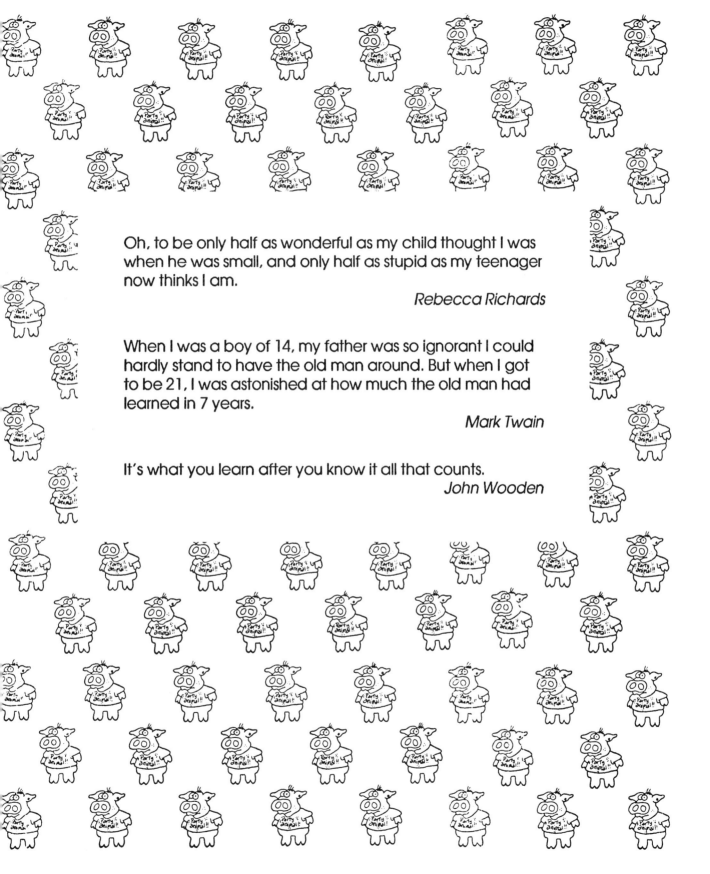

Oh, to be only half as wonderful as my child thought I was when he was small, and only half as stupid as my teenager now thinks I am.

Rebecca Richards

When I was a boy of 14, my father was so ignorant I could hardly stand to have the old man around. But when I got to be 21, I was astonished at how much the old man had learned in 7 years.

Mark Twain

It's what you learn after you know it all that counts.

John Wooden

MOM AND POP QUIZ!!

As the parent of a teenager, you're reasonably mature by now. With maturity comes wisdom. Here's your chance to show off. No cheating. (Only a teenager would cheat, right? Wrong! Take off 1 point if you agreed.)

CHOOSE THE LETTER THAT BEST REPRESENTS THE CORRECT ANSWER.

1. Where do teenagers come from?

    a. Under rocks.
    b. Procreation.
    c. Another planet.
    d. Slave auctions.

2. What is a teenager?

    a. A tax deduction.
    b. An obstinate servant.
    c. A separate human being.
    d. A lower life form than parents.

3. What is a parent?

    a. A saint and martyr.
    b. A doormat.
    c. An infallible being.
    d. A teen's human equal.

4. What is a teen's goal?

    a. Sex, drugs and rock 'n' roll.
    b. To make a parent's life miserable.
    c. To sleep till noon.
    d. To achieve independence and find himself.

5. What is a parent's goal?

a. To survive till teen turns 18.
b. To own and control any human beings they give birth to.
c. To protect teen from himself.
d. To raise an independent, responsible fellow human being.

6. What is the best thing a parent can do for a teen?

a. Disappear from the face of the earth.
b. Let the kid live to see his 18th birthday.
c. Respect teen's independence and let him be responsible for his own actions.
d. Provide a car on his 16th birthday or graduation.

7. Which of the following is the foundation on which your relationship with your teenager is built?

a. Discipline, control and punishments.
b. Your attitude, perception and expectations.
c. Fast cars, big allowances and no curfews.

8. Most of the mistakes you make with your teenager are the direct result of:

a. The depleted ozone layer's effect on your brain.
b. Being too easy or too firm.
c. Not treating your teen with respect.
d. The depleted ozone layer's effect on your teen's brain.

9. Which of the following is most important in changing your teen's behavior and instilling responsibility?

a. Big, tall parents.
b. Letting him experience the consequences of his behavior.
c. Offering him a bigger allowance.
d. Having lots of crystals in the house.

10. The above picture is an example of:

a. Dogs that can read and talk.
b. A mean mommy and a nice, understanding daddy.
c. A daddy owning his teen's problem.

11. Which of the following is considered the "heart and soul" of effective parenting?

a. Consistency.
b. Loving parents.
c. The ability to walk softly and carry a big stick.

12. Which of the following is most crucial for effective communication?

a. A telephone.
b. Listening.
c. Tying the teen to a chair.

ANSWER THE FOLLOWING QUESTIONS TRUE OR FALSE.

13. Teen behavior serves vitally important purposes other than making a parent's life miserable. *T/F*

14. A parent whose motto is "Do as I say, not as I do" can safely expect his teen to do as he says and not as he does. *T/F*

15. Your expectations have very little influence on your teen's life. *T/F*

16. Trust is good, but control has been proved to be more effective. *T/F*

17. All teen misbehaviors occur because of the way you respond to them. *T/F*

18. Retraining a teen involves changing his attitude and the way you interact with him. *T/F*

19. It's not what happens to you in life that affects you; it's how you choose to respond. *T/F*

20. The first few minutes of any encounter are the most critical. *T/F*

21. "I" statements are safer than "you" statements. *T/F*

22. Sometimes all your teen wants is to be heard. *T/F*

23. Listening encourages teens to talk more. *T/F*

24. Your responses can train your teen to talk to you or to tune you out. *T/F*

25. A teen is likely to misbehave or rebel even when he's allowed to negotiate matters that concern him. *T/F*

26. Praise and encouragement are excellent secondary positive consequences to use with your teen. *T/F*

27. A teen should never be allowed to negotiate his own punishment. *T/F*

28. You should pay more attention to the teen's assets and positive behaviors than to his liabilities and screw ups. *T/F*

29. Not getting involved is the best way to deal with certain situations. *T/F*

30. Parenting is serious business, so humor is inappropriate. *T/F*

31. Fighting is an important safety valve in a healthy relationship. *T/F*

32. It's a sign of disrespect and loss of parental control when a teen expresses anger to a parent. *T/F*

33. This is a darn good book, and the artwork is great! *T/F*

34. Don't wean your teen for independence until you feel he's ready for it. *T/F*

35. Giving responsibility encourages a teen to be responsible. *T/F*

ANSWERS TO QUIZ

TAKE THE QUIZ FIRST!, OK?!!

GIVE YOURSELF 1 POINT FOR EACH ANSWER YOU GET CORRECT. GIVE YOURSELF AN EXTRA POINT IF YOU GOT QUESTION 33 RIGHT!!

1. *b.* Procreation (more fun than digging under rocks).
2. *c.* A separate human being. (Did anyone choose tax deduction? A home is a tax deduction, too, but a home is not a teen. Get it?)
3. *d.* A teen's human equal (in most cases).
4. *d.* To achieve independence and find himself. (Some adults are still trying to find themselves.)
5. *d.* To raise independent, responsible kids.
6. *c.* Respect teen's independence, and let him be responsible for his own actions.
7. *b.* Your attitude, perception and expectations.
8. *c.* Not treating your teen with respect (and maybe the ozone, too, who knows?)
9. *b.* Letting him experience the consequences of his behavior.
10. *c.* A daddy owning his teen's problem. (In this case, Mommy knows best!)
11. *a.* Consistency. (Ever heard of misguided love?)
12. *b.* Listening.
13. *T* (Hard to believe, isn't it?)
14. *F* (What a joke.)
15. *F* They have a powerful effect.)
16. *F* (Control is an illusion.)
17. *F* (Some do; some don't.)
18. *F* (It involves changing *your* attitude not his.)
19. *T*
20. *F* (The first few *seconds* are.)
21. *T*
22. *T* (Bad news for know-it-alls and talkaholics.)
23. *T* (Lucky you.)
24. *T*
25. *F* (He's less likely to rebel.)
26. *F* (They're excellent primary positive consequences.)
27. *F* (He'll be more cooperative, so be fair not square!)
28. *T*
29. *T*
30. *F* (Please say you didn't miss this one.)
31. *T* (It's uncomfortable for some, but nevertheless important.)
32. *F*
33. *T* (No doubt about it. This is a darn good book, and the artwork is great.)
34. *F* (All teens must be weaned gradually, even before you think they're ready. Wean on low-risk stuff first.)
35. *T* (So, what are you waiting for? Do it!)

0-10 You're kidding. Only an inanimate object could score this low.

11-15 More scary than a score this low is the type of parent who'd score this low. Shiver. No wonder you're having problems with your teen. You *are* going to reread this book, aren't you?

16-24 This is probably about low-average. Review the sections you flubbed, and you'll score high where it really counts—with your teen.

25-36 Congratulations (excluding all cheaters and lucky guessers)! Considering there were some tricky questions here, you should feel proud of yourself. Now, if you can just incorporate and apply all you've learned consistently and appropriately, you and your teen will both be winners for life.

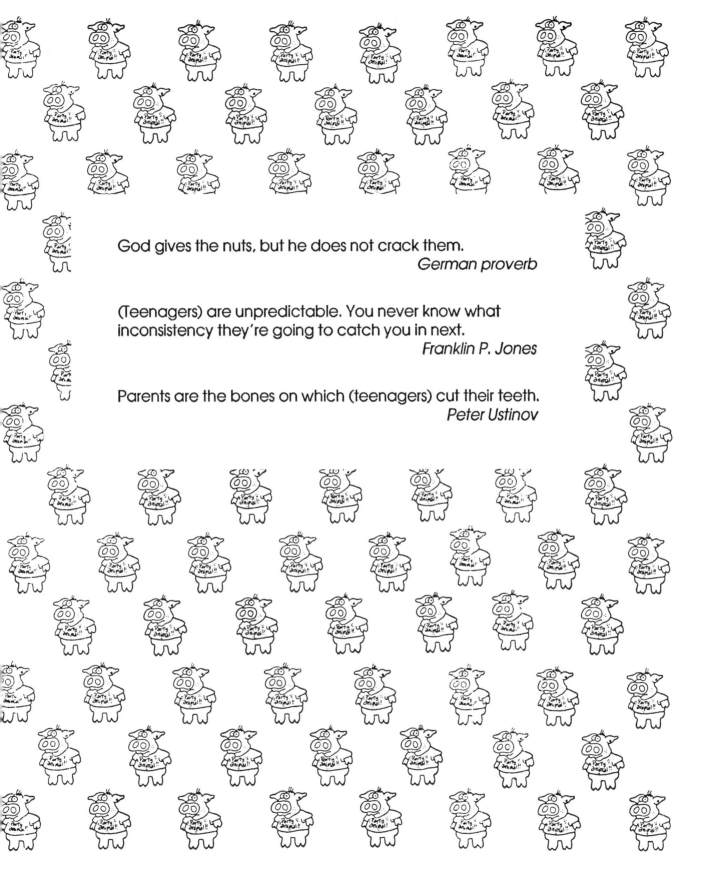

God gives the nuts, but he does not crack them.

German proverb

(Teenagers) are unpredictable. You never know what inconsistency they're going to catch you in next.

Franklin P. Jones

Parents are the bones on which (teenagers) cut their teeth.

Peter Ustinov

THE "NOTHING'S WORKING" CHECKLIST

- ☐ Have you really let go? Are you letting your teen run his own life?
- ☐ Are you encouraging and trusting him to make his own choices?
- ☐ Are you letting him experience the consequences of his own choices?
- ☐ Are you still trying to control behaviors and own his problems?
- ☐ Are you developing a peer relationship based on mutual respect and trust?
- ☐ Have you tailored your expectations to match your teen's interests, abilities and goals, not only your own?

- ☐ Are you overlooking the good in your teen?
- ☐ Are you providing encouragement and praise?

- ☐ Are you remembering to disinvolve yourself from some situations?
- ☐ Are you using good two-way communication skills?
- ☐ Are you responding rationally and non-judgmentally?
- ☐ Have you tried to achieve cooperation by asking his opinion?
- ☐ Are you making parenting a 24-hour-a-day job? (Teens can and should take care of themselves as much as possible.)
- ☐ Have you changed your attitude and the way you choose to respond to his misbehaviors?
- ☐ Are you letting teen misbehavior rob you of your happiness or that of other family members?
- ☐ Are you being too overprotective? Too permissive? Too autocratic?
- ☐ Have you done everything to hassleproof your home/the teen environment?
- ☐ Are you a role model for the kinds of behavior you expect from your teen?
- ☐ Are you remembering to use humor and to smile more?
- ☐ Are you being consistent? Nothing will work if you won't!

NOTE: Certain situations (or teens) are far too tricky or complex for any mortal parent to handle. These call for (drum roll, please) a specialist. Seeking professional counseling is not a sign of parental inadequacy. Rather, it's a sign of caring, commitment and sound mental health. Cars get tune-ups—why not families?

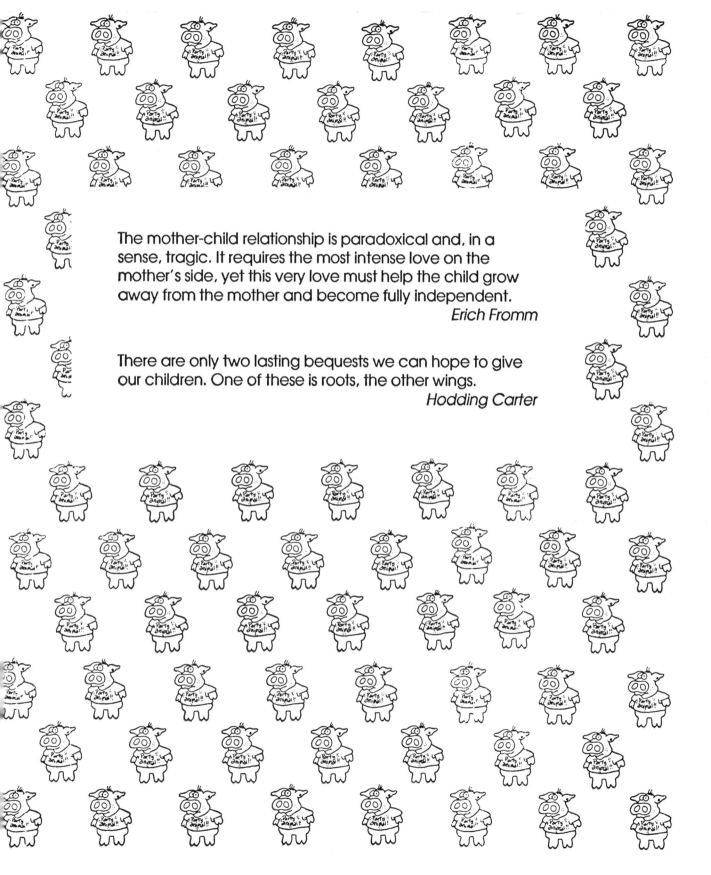

The mother-child relationship is paradoxical and, in a sense, tragic. It requires the most intense love on the mother's side, yet this very love must help the child grow away from the mother and become fully independent.

Erich Fromm

There are only two lasting bequests we can hope to give our children. One of these is roots, the other wings.

Hodding Carter

THE TEEN COMMANDMENTS
(FOR PARENTS)

1. THOU SHALT GET THY ACT TOGETHER AND BE CONSISTENT.

Consistency is the heart and soul of effective parenting. Your inconsistency teaches your teen to misbehave. Teens need to know what to expect. No meaningless threats, no false promises, no random discipline. Mean what you say, say only what you mean and follow through!

2. THOU SHALT BE INDIVISIBLE*.
(* not to be confused with invisibility or birth control.)

Solidarity between parents (even if divorced) is a must. Teens are expert at singling out the weaker parent or playing one against the other. It's "united we stand, or divided we fall." Don't be uncool and fight about the teen or his issues in front of him—he'll feel responsible or see one of you as the hero and one as the villain. Do your negotiating behind closed doors.

3. THOU SHALT LET CONSEQUENCES BE THE HEAVY.

Consequences, not bossy parents, are what makes a teen responsible. They are extremely powerful tools to change or modify behavior. Responsibility can't be taught; it must be given. Consequences can be a payoff for rebellion or an almighty deterrent.

4. THOU SHALT LOVE AND RESPECT THY TEENAGER AS THYSELF.

Your teen is a separate person of equal human worth, not chattel. Treat him the way you'd want to be treated or at least as good as your friends. They who are not busy fighting are busy not fighting (enjoying each other).

5. THOU SHALT ACCEPT THY PARENTAL LIMITATIONS.

Change what you can or should change, and accept what you can't change (or control). And pray you'll be wise enough to distinguish which is which for your teen's sake and your own. (Think of the money you'll save on aspirin and antacids.)

6. THOU SHALT NOT COVET THY TEENAGER'S RESPONSIBILITIES AND PROBLEMS.

It's enough of a hassle to run one life (your own) much less try and run your teen's life, too. Your duty to yourself and your teen is to allow him to become increasingly responsible for the consequences and headaches of running his own life.

7. THOU SHALT NOT PRETEND TO BE INFALLIBLE.

Who are you kidding? You're human. You know it, and your teen knows it. Make your mistakes but be a role model. Own up to mistakes and apologize. Your teen will admire you and overlook your flaws (hopefully)!

8. THOU SHALT NOT BEAR FALSE GUILT.

Don't buy any tickets for any guilt trips, and don't let anyone sell you any, either. Don't blame yourself for things you can't control or aren't responsible for. (That's your teen's job.)

9. THOU SHALT TAKE TIME OFF TO SMELL THY ROSES.

Ease up. You're taking this job of parenting far too seriously! Feel free to be yourself. Punch out on the parenting time clock once in awhile. Let your teen see the real you.

10. THOU SHALT NOT BE A SOURPUSS.

You can catch more teenage flies with honey and humor than vinegar and sour grapes. Look for every appropriate opportunity to avert or diffuse a situation through love and authentic humor (but not hidden anger via sarcasm). Let love and humor be your first resort. The family that hugs and laughs, lasts!

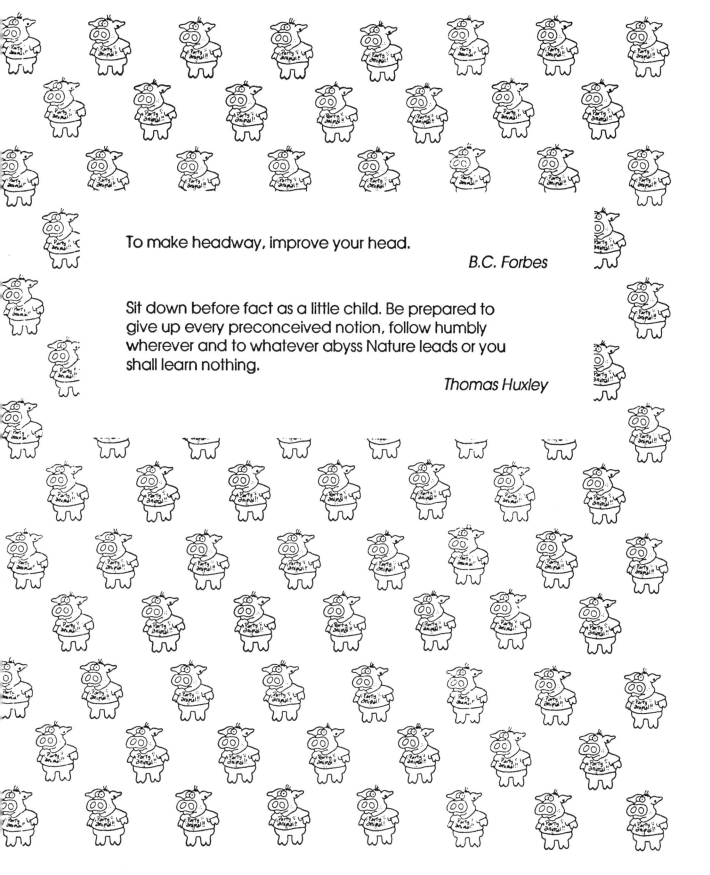

To make headway, improve your head.

B.C. Forbes

Sit down before fact as a little child. Be prepared to give up every preconceived notion, follow humbly wherever and to whatever abyss Nature leads or you shall learn nothing.

Thomas Huxley

General

Bradshaw, John. *The Family*. Deerfield Beach, Florida: Health Communications, Inc., 1988. (Also available on audio and videocassettes.) This is must reading!

Peck, Scott M. *The Road Less Traveled*. New York: Simon & Schuster, Inc., 1978.

Alcohol/Drugs

Forrest, G.G. *How to Cope with a Teenage Drinker: New Alternatives and Hope for Parents and Families*. New York: Atheneum, 1983.

Hyden, Nancy. *If Your Child Is Drinking*. Woodward, New York: G.P. Putnam's Sons, 1981.

Van Ost, William C. M.D., F.A.A.P., and Van Ost, Elaine. *Warning Signs—A Parent's Guide to In-Time Intervention in Drug & Alcohol Abuse*. New York: Warner Books, 1988.

Delinquency/Runaways

Falkin, Gregory P. *Reducing Delinquency: A Strategic Planning Approach*. Lexington, Massachusetts: Lexington Books, 1979.

Madison, Arnold. *Runaway Teens: An American Tragedy*. New York: Elsevier/Nelson Books, 1979.

Divorce/Stepfamilies

Ricci, Isolina. *Mom's House/Dad's House: Making Shared Custody Work*. New York: Macmillan Publishing Co., Inc., 1980.

Visher, Emily B. and Visher, John S. *How to Win as a Stepfamily*. New York: Dembner Books, 1982.

Eating Disorders

Boskind-White, Marlene and White, William C. *Bulimarexia: The Binge/Purge Cycle*. New York: W.W. Norton and Co., 1983.

Palmer, Richard L. *Anorexia Nervosa: A Guide for Sufferers and Their Families*. New York: Penguin Books, 1980.

School

Nielsen, Linda. *How to Motivate Adolescents: A Guide for Parents, Teachers and Counselors*. Englewood Cliffs, New Jersey: Prentice-Hall, Inc., 1982.

Sexuality/Pregnancy

Bell, Ruth. *Changing Bodies, Changing Lives*. New York: Vintage Books, 1988.

Hass, Aaron. *Teenage Sexuality*. New York: Macmillan Publishing Co., Inc., 1979.

Oettinger, Katherine B. with Mooney, E.C. *Not My Daughter: Facing Up to Adolescent Pregnancy*. New York: St. Martin's Press, 1980.

Suicide/Depression

Abraham, Regina. *Teenage Depression and Suicide*. New York: Chelsea House Publishers, 1986.

Griffin, Mary and Felsenthal, Carol. *A Cry for Help: Exploring and Exploding the Myths about Teenage Suicide—A Guide for All Parents of Adolescents*. New York: Doubleday & Co., 1983.

Don't forget:

✓ Professional Counseling. Invaluable even if you think you don't *need* it.

✓ Hotlines, Special Interest Groups. Check yellow pages for 24-hour hotlines and agencies/ groups both locally and nationally.

Bayard, Robert and Bayard, Jean. *How to Deal with Your Acting-Up Teenager.* M. Evans and Co., 1981.

Beck, Irene. "Teen Anger—Limits on Freedom Often Are the Trigger." *The Tucson Citizen,* Tucson, Arizona, 10/27/87.

Bettelheim, Bruno (interviewed by Elisabeth Hall). "Our Children Are Treated Like Idiots." *Psychology Today,* July, 1981. pp. 28-44.

Cantor, Pamela. "Powerful Myth of the Perfect Mother." *The Los Angeles Times,* 9/13/87.

Corey, Gerald. *Theory and Practice of Counseling and Psychotherapy.* Brooks/Cole, 1977.

Csikszentmihalyi, Mihaly and Larson, Reed. *Being Adolescent—Conflict and Growth in the Teenage Years.* Basic Books, Inc., 1984.

Dinkmeyer, Don and McKay, Gary D. *The Parent's Guide—The STEP Approach to Parenting Your Teenager.* American Guidance Service, Inc., 1983.

Dodson, Fitzhugh. *How to Discipline with Love.* Signet, 1977.

Dreikurs, Rudolf and Grey, Loren. *A Parent's Guide to Child Discipline.* Hawthorn/Dutton, 1968.

Faber, Adele and Mazlish, Elaine. *How to Talk so Kids Will Listen & Listen so Kids Will Talk.* Avon, 1980.

Fontenelle, Don H., *How to Live With Your Children.* Fisher Books, 1989.

Friel, John and Friel, Linda. *Adult Children: The Secrets of Dysfunctional Families.* Health Communications, Inc., 1988.

Ginott, Haim G., *Between Parent & Teenager.* Avon. 1969.

Gould, Shirley. *Teenagers: The Continuing Challenge.* E.P. Dutton, 1987.

Gordon, Thomas, *P.E.T.—Parent Effectiveness Training.* Plume Books, 1970.

Hersch, Patricia. "The Perils of Rock 'n' Roll." *Psychology Today,* September 1987, page 80.

Kolodny, Robert C. and Nancy J., Bratter, Thomas and Deep, Cheryl. *How to Survive Your Adolescent's Adolescence.* Little, Brown, 1984.

McKenzie, Thomas. "You're Not Alone When Your Kids Reject You," *U.S. Catholic,* July, 1981, pp. 1-18.

Miller, Alice. *Thou Shalt Not Be Aware: Society's Betrayal of the Child.* Meridian, 1986.

Peck, Scott M., M.D., *The Road Less Traveled.* Simon & Schuster, Inc., 1978.

Perry, James. A. "Survival Kits Assist Parents of Adolescents." *The Times-Picayune,* New Orleans, Louisiana, 10/8/87.

Peterson, Karen S. "Kids Saying to Parents: 'I Need You.'" *U.S.A. Today,* 5/24/87.

Rosemond, John. "When You Disapprove of Your Teenager's Pals." *Better Homes and Gardens,* August, 1987, page 48.

Slaikeu, Karl A., Ph.D. "Mediation Model," The Center for Conflict Management, Inc., 1986.

Steinberg, Laurence. "Bound to Bicker." *Psychology Today,* September, 1987, pp. 36-39.

Thompson, Barbara. "Teaching Children Responsibility." *The Tucson Citizen,* Tucson, Arizona, 4/14/87.

Ubell, Earl. "Should You Spare the Rod?" *Parade Magazine,* 8/2/87.

Weinhaus, Evonne and Friedman, Karen. *Stop Struggling with Your Teen.* J. B. Speck Press, 1984.

Westin, Jeane. *The Coming Parent Revolution.* Rand McNally, 1981.

ABOUT THE AUTHOR !!! ...

Beverly Guhl is an insightful mother of two teenagers. A commercial artist with a worldwide reputation, Beverly's delightful designs and characters have appeared on greeting cards, bookmarks, mugs, magnets and other products in the US and England. Additionally, she has done record-album covers, co-authored an animated video for children and licensed her posters. Her first book, *Purrfect Parenting* (also published by Fisher Books), is a guide for parents of young children.